The Excellence
of Faith

DR. NOSAYABA EVBUOMWAN

authorHOUSE®

AuthorHouse™
1663 Liberty Drive
Bloomington, IN 47403
www.authorhouse.com
Phone: 1 (800) 839-8640

Published by AuthorHouse 06/12/2018

ISBN: 978-1-5462-3952-9 (sc)
ISBN: 978-1-5462-3950-5 (hc)
ISBN: 978-1-5462-3951-2 (e)

Library of Congress Control Number: 2018905038

Print information available on the last page.

This book is printed on acid-free paper.

Dedication

This book is dedicated to my Lord and Saviour Jesus Christ, whose love, mercy, grace, favour, miracles and faithfulness continues to amaze me.

This book is also dedicated to men and women who despite all odds and challenges of life, have remained steadfast in faith and not given up on God.

Many men and women of God have impacted my life of faith, notably Archbishop Benson A Idahosa, Bishop J.B.S. Coker, Rev. Felix Omobude, Dr. Omadeli Boyo, Kenneth E Hagin (Snr), Bishop Margaret Wangari (Nairobi, Kenya) and my wife Dr Anne Olufunmilayo Evbuomwan.

Acknowledgements

My special thanks go to my able and loving wife Dr Anne Olufunmilayo Evbuomwan for her continuous encouragement and support during the writing of this book.

Many thanks are due to my friend and co-labourer Pastor Taiwo Ayeni, for his meticulous editing, suggestions and formatting.

An especial thanks to my brother, friend and classmate Reverend Doctor Ode Andrew Eyeoyibo, a wordsmith par excellence for agreeing to write the foreword for this book within 24hrs.

The initial transcription work by Pastor George Idagbe from my audio messages of the series taught on this subject is gratefully acknowledged.

Many thanks are due Olusegun Sam Olayinka who edited the initial audio message series and coordinated the transcription and typing of the draft manuscript. Nancy Cervantez and Shwan Lee, volunteers/ community workers at Eagle Believers International Church, Lewisville, Texas who played a significant role in the initial typing of the handwritten transcription are sincerely appreciated.

Foreword

The book, 'The Excellence of Faith' is a book about "mere faith". Not, 'mere' now as in ordinary, insubstantial and unimportant, but used in the C. S. Lewisian sense- as used in his book, Mere Christianity- as the heart, substance, essence and skeletal structure of faith. It is a book that has everything. It has world history, church history, theology, biblical studies, exegesis and practical pastoral exhortation. It is a book laden with testimonies not just of biblical and other generational heroes but also of the writer. It is a human story; a living, breathing and vital document. Nosa being a mathematician and an engineer will be expected to deploy the language of numbers to establish his points, but surprisingly he more ably deploys the Grammarian's art. He talks about the adjectives, pronouns, nouns and prepositions of faith. He deploys philosophical language by talking about the propositions of faith. Yet this is not an inaccessible book that can only be read by scholars. He uses short, punchy sentences in a manner that puts me in mind of Hemingway. He tells stories; he is very anecdotal. He deals with fear and lack and shortage. He does not shy away from talking about the vexed question of money. He establishes the irreducible minimums of our faith or of 'the faith' (the Didache) as he puts. Faith in God as Father, Jesus as Son and the Holy Ghost as comforter. A biblical faith, it goes without saying. This book is a readable feast. It's a table laden with victuals and scriptural vignettes and set before both friend and foe. The language is felicitous and clement. It is not strident even when stating some very barefaced and seemingly controversial distinctives of the faith. It's a book about both the tenets and the practice of faith. Not faith taught behind the verdant walls of a seminary. But a lived in lived out faith rooted in an encounter with the God of faith, the Lord of faith and the Spirit of faith. This book is a comprehensive compendium of the Christian life which though focused on faith, takes in other broad themes of hope, love, the new creation in Christ, living a holy life and more and more. It could have been titled, Growing up spiritually. The exposition on Hebrews 11 by itself justifies the price of this book. In reading through the book I literally felt my faith growing and expanding. I must stop, so that you can quickly get to the main event- the reading of the book. It's literally unputdownable, because of the flow of the narrative and the urgency and primacy of the matters canvassed within. If the just shall live by their faith as the book tells us they are enjoined four times, then the importance of this book cannot in any case be overstated. Please read it, devour it and purchase many copies as gifts.

Reverend Doctor Ode Andrew Eyeoyibo
Senior Pastor
Ezra House- a word of love Church
Akowonjo, Lagos Nigeria.

CONTENTS

INTRODUCTION

John introducing his epistle in 1 John 1:1 declares:

"[I am writing about] what existed from the beginning, what we have heard, what we have seen with our eyes, what we looked at and touched with our hands..."

We live in a generation that is questioning God's word and the reality of the truth that we believe. In discussing **the excellence of the Christian faith**, just like apostle John, this author would be sharing from, not just a theological and/or belief system, but also from a practical, evidence and experience based perspective. God is the origin of the faith we have and He is the central focus of the discussion of faith.

Why is the Christian faith supreme?

Christians need to stand up for what they believe and not bow in defeat. I admit that I have strong convictions in and about the Lord Jesus Christ. As part of my core faith and belief system, I love everyone; I love humanity, irrespective of race, status, gender, sexual orientation, or any other categorization. I can hang out with any of them. Like Paul said, I personally *"...know both how to be abased, and I know how to abound...."* (Phil 4:12). My love for every human being makes it incumbent on me to tell the truth.

Our most holy faith is what I call the adjective of faith. There is one faith, and it's known as the faith. Faith is a real spiritual force that produces tangible results. This is one reason we can talk about heroes of faith in Hebrews 11. The kind of works they did through faith was so outstanding that Church historians tagged the protagonists in Hebrews 11 as Heroes of Faith. We are counseled in Jude 20 about "*...building up yourself on your most holy faith...*" What is this faith? It is the God kind of faith.

Let me begin by declaring that everyone has faith. Even Atheists too have faith. They just have faith in themselves and spend time exercising faith in the notion of the non-existence of God. So we all have faith. Faith in a general sense, is what you believe. Like when you sit on a chair, you believe that it will not collapse under you or when you get inside your car you believed before you cranked the engine that it was going to start. That doesn't necessarily mean you are exercising the Christian faith. **So there is no faith vacuum - everyone exercises faith.** Everyone has some level of faith, but for Christians, our faith is based on the word of God; it is based on the Triune God.

If you are a Christian, you must know that there is God the Father, God the Son, and God the Holy Spirit. You can't say you're a Christian if you do not believe in the Triune God. We know there is God the father who made and created the world, God the son who came to die for us, and God the Holy Spirit who indwells and empowers us through grace.

Right now Jesus Christ who used to walk on the shores of Jerusalem is not here, so how do you know you believe in the real Jesus? No matter the questions or doubts running through your minds, we know He is here by His spirit, and also the fact that the Holy Spirit dwells in us. We carry Him to our homes, our cars and everywhere. In addition, we know that the manifest presence of the Lord Jesus Christ in our midst is demonstrated by the active work of the Holy Spirit.

Our faith is based on the foundational truth that God the Father is going to judge the world by Jesus Christ, God the Son. My faith is not just based on the fact that I go to church, or my family are Christians, therefore I'm a Christian. Your faith must be based on the truth of the existence of the Triune God; God the father, God the Son, and God the Holy Spirit. This is the faith that is rooted in God, or we can call it **rooted faith.**

I believe that the Christian faith is supreme, and there is an excellence about it. This is the premise of this book, which attempts to give a balance treatise to the subject of the Christian faith.

The book begins with an exploration of the subject of Our Most Holy Faith. In the second chapter, the phrase "The Just shall live by faith" is comprehensively examined on the basis of foundational principles. The purpose and rationale for faith is discussed extensively in Chapter 3. The fourth chapter discusses the pronouns of faith - that is the fact that our faith is personal. You cannot solely depend on someone else's faith; you have to have your own faith to operate here on earth.

The prepositions of faith, - that is, faith is tangible and not guess work is elucidated in chapter 5. Hebrews 11 forms the basis for the discussion of some of the Heroes of Faith in Chapter 6. Types and levels of faith and hindrances to Faith form the subjects of Chapters 7 and 8 respectively. Important key attributes of faith are discussed in Chapter 9 and Chapter 10 discusses in a step by step fashion, living by faith from a practical perspective. The book concludes on the truth that biblical Faith ONLY works by LOVE.

CHAPTER 1

Our Most Holy Faith

THE word 'the' is a definite article that helps to describe the word 'faith' as unique state of things. In general, everyone believes or has faith in something. For the celebrated Atheists, one can say they believe or have faith in themselves. There is no faith vacuum. The spirit of man wants to and does have faith in a person or thing. The basis of many religious groups is the belief in a higher power called by several names in these groups. So the word faith is commonly used to represent one's belief and practices.

Everyone has some form of faith, and faith in a general sense is what you believe. Like sitting on a chair and believing it will not collapse under you. This is not necessarily the Christian faith. For the Christian, our foundational faith is in the Triune God, namely God the Father, God the Son and God the Holy Spirit. This faith is completely based on the integrity of the Bible from which the canons of the Christian belief system are derived. The Christian believes in God the Father as the creator of all things including heaven and earth, in God the Son as savior and Lord who was manifested (incarnated) in human flesh to die as a substitute for our sins and in God the Holy Spirit who indwells every believer in Christ today, and directs their activities in line with the will of God.

Right now Jesus is not here, so how do you know you believe in the real Jesus? No matter the questions or doubts running through your mind, we know He is with us by His spirit. We also have the evidence of His indwelling presence in us, and He is with us everywhere. The reason I can make this declaration is that since giving my life to Christ, I have fought many battles, gone through many valleys, and climbed many mountains yet; I am still rooted in Jesus. The Christian faith may not be visible, but it cannot be defeated and that is what many Christians need to learn.

Some Christians are ignorant of this faith. They look at a man or a woman and they reduce his or her Christian life to who they look like now, have now or their current status in life. They lack an understanding of what the Lord Jesus said in John 3:8:

"The wind bloweth where it listeth, and thou hearest the sound thereof, but canst not tell whence it cometh, and whither it goeth: so is every one that is born of the Spirit."

We do not have an idea of a person's total lot in life, and therefore we should stop trying to predict. It's the Lord who has that prerogative, and we must understand that. We must also be careful in this regard, because our faith is rooted in the Lord. That is why Jesus in His word encourages believers to make sure that our hearts are not like the wayside, thorny or stony ground, but the good ground where the word of God can effectively grow and bring forth much fruit.

In addition, the Christian faith is absolute and completely dogmatic about the reality and tangibility of God. This faith believes in a Living God who is actively involved in our lives. It believes in the All powerful, All knowing and a universally present God, with whom we have an intimate relationship and fellowship. This faith is not temporal, it is eternal, and it has a permanence that continues in the life beyond the present. This faith deliberately works and partners with the Living God in actualizing His plans and purposes on the earth. No wonder Jude calls it "*...your Most Holy Faith...*" (Jude verse 20).

Many non-Christians often have a challenge with regards to the definiteness and absoluteness of the Christian faith. What does that mean? Jesus is the only way. Some people don't like to hear that, but the truth is Jesus is the only way. An example is the case of one of the founding ministers of our local church, Eagle Believers International church, who is now a pastor in downtown Dallas, Texas. He came to America as a Muslim, and lived at that time in Arlington, Texas. One day a young girl looked at him and said "You serve a fake prophet!" And for three days he could not sleep. The thought troubled him until he surrendered his life to Jesus.

After he got saved, one-night demon spirits came to attack him, and that night he didn't remember Allah, but he remembered Jesus who showed up for him. That is why he is on fire for Jesus till today and he runs a church ministry to the homeless in South Dallas.

Don't let your friends deceive you. Jesus is the only Way, the only Truth and the only Life – (John 14:6). No Jesus, no life and He is the answer for the world. The God we serve is not mere philosophy, He is true and real! If He is just mere philosophy, then there is no point worshiping Him. He is a tangible and real God. He has eyes, ears, mouth, hands and legs. I am sure you must have read from the Bible metaphorical statements about the finger of God, or the hand of God?

You have to personally know beyond any reasonable doubt that your God is a living God. I thank God no matter what I have been through, I never have to doubt the reality of God. In my entire Christian life, God has done things for me that only He alone could have done, and you cannot convince me otherwise. I saw grace, as a young man that I knew it was beyond me. So I know, this is not about me, this is about the God who can interfere in the affairs of men.

For example, when I got saved, I could read for a few hours that I had, and understood what I previously read for many hours. You cannot tell me that that is mere human intelligence, - that's God's grace at work. For your information there is super intelligence from God, and He can bless your memory, finances, health, and do something that no one else can do. This is why it is important that your faith be rooted in that kind of God. Paul said in 1 Corinthians 2:1-5 that:

"And I, brethren, when I came to you, came not with excellency of speech or of wisdom, declaring unto you the testimony of God.

For I determined not to know anything among you, save Jesus Christ, and him crucified.

And I was with you in weakness, and in fear, and in much trembling.

And my speech and my preaching was not with enticing words of man's wisdom, but in demonstration of the Spirit and of power:

That your faith should not stand in the wisdom of men, but in the power of God."

We see Paul here showing he always determined, desired and sought for the manifestation of the power of God in all of his preaching. It is a necessity for God to confirm the preaching of His word with signs following (Mark 16:20).

For this reason, your faith must be firm, dogmatic and rooted in God. This is the kind of faith that believes in the Living God, and who is active in your life. Some people may question your faith in a God you don't see, but don't be put off. You may not see Him, but He is active in your life and that should be sufficient evidence for you. He's not far from you. He hears your prayers. He is with you when you wake up in the morning, at your job, and when you return home.

Our faith is rooted in the all powerful God (Omni-Potent), the all knowing God (Omni-Scient., the God, who is everywhere – (Omni-Present). The God that knows everything and He is the all powerful God and no matter what you are going through in life, God can change it. That's why the Lord Jesus said in Mark II: 22

"Have faith in God".

God is active, and He's involved in our lives and not restricted by distance or location.

"For whatsoever is born of God overcomes the world: and this is the victory that overcomes the world, even our faith" (1 John 5:4).

When I was in Africa, He was with me and I overcame. When I went to Europe, I overcame there too, and I possessed the land. It was not because of me, it was because of who I carried, and whose I am. Don't be intimidated by the system in the US and the world. You can possess the land in this country and anywhere God places you. The reason is that the Bible says in 2 Corinthians 4:7 that: *"...we have this treasure in earthen vessels that the Excellency of the power may be of him."*

Exercising this individual faith in the finished work of the Lord Jesus Christ on the cross, His burial and resurrection, results in a transformed and audacious life as a Son of God (John 1:12). You then become a new creation of God (2 Corinthians 5:17) and recreated being, made alive and born again by the Spirit of God - (John 1:13 and John 3:1-8). It is a Holy Faith, because it sets you apart from the world system and unto God as one of His peculiar people (1 Peter 2:9).

Many of us need to understand that being born again is not about just going to church, it is more and it is about carrying divinity, and the life of God within us. It is an overcoming life. Where ever you go, you will overcome. For example, in the 1980's as a teenager I went with a group to a village outreach, and confronted witches and wizards in their shrines. After praying both in tongues and our understanding, at the end of that evening, the chief priest said these people have disconnected me from my medium. Beloved, don't be afraid the power of God in you can do the impossible but we must exercise our faith to do exploits for Him. The strength behind these exploits is because our faith is not temporary, but permanent and anchored in the Lord Jesus Christ. Paul says in 1 Corinthians 15:19:

"If only in this world you have hope in God, you are of all men most miserable".

The blessings of God inspired by this faith are not limited to this world alone, it transcends the earth. That is why your Christian faith should not just be about getting material things - house, car, job, wife or husband. Yes, God will bless you with a house, car, job, wife or husband but the Christian faith involves much more than that and it is not just only for or about things. However, this is where many people are, and it is what I call one sided Christianity. These ones are like Ephraim, a cake not turned (Hosea 7:8). They only know the God that provides material things; that is, the "give me, give me" God. So the day that God doesn't give them what they want, they walk out on Him. They only know about the hand of God, like the Israelites who only knew the acts of God, but not His ways (Psalm 103:7).

This faith is not temporary and so don't be tempted to think the day you don't see things happen, that means God is not there again. You better believe it, He's with us forever and "***Whosoever believes in Him shall not perish but have everlasting life.***" (John 3:16).

Our God has no beginning and no ending. His relationship with us is not just for here. The faith you live now will transcend into the life after death. If you don't believe Jesus is coming again, then you can take your Bible as just another book. If you don't believe there is life after death, then why are you a Christian? There is life after death and your life does not end here.

In fact, the kingdom we don't see is greater than the one we see. There are people who have died, went to heaven and came back. One of the most outstanding things I have heard them say was that they saw colors that they have not seen here on earth and heard sounds of music they have never heard before. There is nothing here compared with the beauty of heaven. For this reason, many of them prayed not to come back. However, some of them came back because their loved ones prayed to God to please release them back to them, and God did.

There are also testimonies of some unbelievers who saw heaven, came back to the earth, repented and vowed never to miss heaven. The lives of those who were already Christians changed. Their attitude to life changed, the things that used to move them don't move them anymore because they were thinking of the life beyond here.

Our faith is for the life beyond which has an eternal hope and that is "...*Christ in you, the hope of glory:*" (Colossians 1:27). Our faith has a hope rooted in Christ, and this truly is our life. It is about life here and hereafter. This is about when Jesus comes, where will you be? When your life on earth is ended and you stand before the white throne judgment, what is going to happen? This is one reason why your faith must not be a mediocre one. It must not be a casual one or a joke.

This faith has cost people their lives, their families and their entire wealth. This faith has eternal hope, and it is very deliberate. This means our faith deliberately works and partners with the living God. Let me explain. You are not an accident on the earth, God invested in you, and partnered with you to fulfill an assignment for Him here on earth. You're one of you, and you are the only one like you which is why if you fail, it is a colossal failure. So it is not enough to say, "Hallelujah, I am born again, and filled with the Holy Ghost, Amen. Blessed be the name of the Lord." Then thereafter you sit down. No. But that's what a majority of Christians are doing today, however, you must step out into His purpose for your life.

Many of us Christians are saved, but we don't move on to what I call Stewardship and allow the Lordship of Jesus Christ to dominate our lives. We need to take ownership of the kingdom, and see it as our own. I believe that part of the works of my faith in God is to take ownership in His Kingdom. Any church I've ever been in Africa, in Europe and here in the US, I have engaged intensely with them as my Father's business and hence received it as mine. I care about Jesus who saved me. I am a servant not of a church, or a denomination but a servant of Jesus Christ, so I take ownership of the kingdom. I don't care what denomination you are in, for as long as you are in Christ, you are my brother or sister. That is what the Bible teaches and I truly believe it.

This faith partners with God, so when I come into a city, or a local church, my first thought must be, Lord what would you have me to do? What is it that I am supposed to do to advance your purpose? So when I pay my tithes and offerings, it's not for the pastor, it is so that meat may be available for the kingdom use. For some of us it is a matter of where your heart is that is where your treasure is. I want to challenge you, change the focus of your treasure to the kingdom of God. If it is dependent on the church, the body of Christ will not be where we are today. Whether in Africa, Europe, or anywhere we will not be where we are, if those who call themselves Christians invest in the kingdom.

The faith we have and our resources must be released in and to the kingdom. It must be used to partner with God. Do you know why Jesus was so successful? One word and it is in Psalm 40:7-8: "...*Lo, I come: in the volume of the book it is written of me, I delight to do thy will, O my God...*".

So there is a will of God for your life. There are faith partners with Him, to accomplish the will of God. Your will is not my will, and the call of God for you is not the call of God for me. That is why I have no time to waste analyzing people. I just focus on myself.

I need to succeed in what God has called me to do. The calling of God on my life is what I am called to do. I must partner in this faith. What about you? What has God called you to do? Why are you on earth? Do you know why you are on earth? Do you know why you are in the City or country that you are right now? Do you know why you are in the church you are in? Have you answered those questions? They are questions you must answer for you to move on in your Christian faith. That is why Jude calls it *"Our most holy faith"* (Jude 20).

In fact, Christianity is not a religion and it is not a way of life either. Christianity is life. Christianity is Jesus. Do you have Jesus? No Jesus, no life. That's the bottom line. So our faith is a holy faith, that is, a set apart faith. This most holy and indeed elevated faith is realized when we come to know God as the one and only true God and Jesus Christ whom He sent to redeem us. Succinctly, the Lord Jesus Christ said in John 17:3:

"This is life eternal, that they might know thee, the only true God, and Jesus Christ whom thou hast sent."

The Lord Jesus is central to this faith, and it is based on eternal life. It is the faith that believes in the only true God, and there is only one true God. Every other God is a false God, and they are creatures of men. Whoever is not the God of Jesus is a false God. You may ask me, who is the true God? He is the father of Jesus. If you are not the father of Jesus, then you are a false God. This faith which is indeed "THE FAITH" believes that the God, who sent Jesus Christ into the world, is the ONLY true God.

And John 1:12 tells us:

"For as many as received him, to them he gave power to become the sons of God" (John 1:12).

This faith, I am writing about, works by love and it's true and eternal. The true faith works by love (Galatians 5:6). Our faith is supreme because it is based on love, giving and forgiving others. If I say I am a child of God, my modus operandi and principal way to operate should always be by love. So in everything I say or do, the question I should ask myself is, "Is this motivated by love?" When you gossip about that brother or sister, is that love? When you hold grudges against somebody in your heart, is that love? When you won't greet that brother, is that love? That's not the faith of God.

This faith works by love. Your faith is only as powerful as your love life, and it cannot produce result for you unless it is love based, and operated and rooted through love. It is not based on hate, selfishness, pride, arrogance, but is rooted in love. So if I truly love God, I should love God's people. This I call the cross of Love. For this reason, you must examine your Christianity, like Paul said in 2 Corinthians 13:5 *"...test whether you are still in the faith"*.

What drives you as a Christian or what motivates you? Is it self-aggrandizement or the love of God? There must be no doubt in your mind that Jesus came to this world as a man, that He died as a man and He rose again. He's alive; if you ever doubt the resume of Jesus then your faith is faulty. If you are confused about that, read 1 Corinthian 15, study it and look at the argument of Paul the attorney about resurrection. If Jesus be not risen, you are wasting your time following Him.

There must be no doubt in your mind that He rose again. I went to Israel in 2001 with my wife and I saw His empty tomb. You don't have to go to Israel to believe. I had already believed before I went to Israel, and didn't have to see the empty tomb to believe. Jesus changed my life and that is how I know that He's alive. He transformed me, gave me peace, and joy unspeakable. Our faith must be audacious and based on the Son of God. This faith is based on the regeneration that Jesus does as stated in 2 Corinthians 5:17. That is our faith, and it believes in a transformed life where we are changed from being a sinner to a saint. When you are born again you are a new creation, you are a saint of God because the Bible says: *"For he hath made him to be sin for us, who knew no sin; that we might be made the righteousness of God in him."* (2 Corinthians 5:21)

He has imputed unto you His righteousness that though He had no sin, yet He became sin that you may become righteous. There was an

exchange. This fact Colossians 1:13 clearly expressed that God "...
***delivered us from the power of darkness, and hath translated us
into the kingdom of his dear Son:"***

When you are not born again, you are under the jurisdiction of the devil,
but the day you get born again, you are translated into the kingdom of
God's dear son. The biggest deception of the devil is to make you believe
that you are still under his jurisdiction or control and therefore nothing
has changed. The truth is you're in God's kingdom, but your mind is
still thinking about the world and your sinful ways.

Remember how the Israelites resisted Moses, saying leave us alone? Do
you want to kill us in the wilderness? You know when a Christian gets
born again, and start having problems; he or she will say "I shouldn't
have become a Christian, when I was an unbeliever I never used to have
this kind of problems." The reason you think this way is because your
mind has not been renewed.

As a believer, to overcome the temptations, you have to reckon yourself
dead indeed unto sin and alive to God (Romans 6:11). You were a slave
to sin; but you have now become a slave to righteousness. That's what
Romans chapter 6 teaches us. If you are in Christ there is a newness of
life, you are born again and there must be evidence. That's why James
challenged the early church Christians, don't be saying you are Christians
by mouth, but show me your faith by your works (James 2:18).

You are not saved by works. Salvation is by grace that is the root. If
you have the root, we must see the fruit. If you have Jesus as your root,
then show us the fruit of Jesus or your works. That's what James was
saying, and by them you produce the evidence that truly something has
happened in your life. How did I know I had become a Christian? I
took a pen and paper; I wrote a letter of apology to two of my classmates
whom I quarreled with. No pastor taught me this, yet I was just fourteen
years old. When something has happened inside you, there would be
outward physical evidence. So if any man be in Christ, he's a new

creation. This holy faith sets you apart as: *"...a chosen generation, a royal priesthood, an holy nation, a peculiar people...."* (1 Peter 2:9).

Furthermore, you are set apart to: *"...shew forth the praises of him who hath called you out of darkness into his marvelous light..."* Therefore, you cannot behave like your friends who are still unbelievers. I know you work in the same hospital, school, or accounting office, but you're a Christian now. There must be evidence that you're a peculiar person unto God.

The standard for your faith walk should not be set by the news media or the culture of the society and those who contradict you. You must know the scriptures to build a solid foundation for your faith. We are enjoined in 2 Timothy 2:15 to:

"Study to shew thyself approved unto God, a workman that needeth not to be ashamed, rightly dividing the word of truth."

You cannot afford to be an uneducated Christian, because the knowledge of your faith and convictions would be challenged, and you must always *"...be ready always to give an answer to every man that asketh you a reason of the hope that is in you with meekness and fear:* (1 Peter 3:15)

It is disappointing that there are too many uneducated Christians out there. They don't know the bible, and therefore don't know the truth. So they can easily be lied to and swayed in the wrong direction. When I was confronted about the gospel, I looked at the bible. I also reviewed my history text book because at that point, I wasn't so sure, that, Jesus was not a fairy tale. The history text books revealed there was a man called Jesus Christ and He was in Israel and He died and they said "he rose again". So history confirmed to me what the bible says about Jesus is true.

So I first of all started from history, and then looked at the bible. However, the more I read the bible the more I realized that the bible is true, and that my faith is not a blind faith. Many years ago, I read a very intelligent journalist, Lee Strobel, who wanted to dispute the veracity of Christianity, but the more he researched, the more problem he faced in proving that there is no God. The testimony is that in the process, before he could finish the first book he became a born again Christian. He has at this time written many books, about evidence of faith that we have and experience.

The story of Josh McDowell, who in his search for true faith met Christ, is worth mentioning here also. His search began as a teenager when he was pressured to find answers to three basic questions "Who am I? Why am I here? Where am I going?" In the final analysis, his compilations of his discoveries were documented in a series of books titled 'Evidence that Demands a Verdict'. In his own words "I had to admit that Jesus Christ was more than a carpenter. He was all he claimed to be."

So my beloved readers, our most Holy faith is not a blind faith. It has evidential basis in history, archaeology, nature, natural and physical sciences as well as in the word of God. It is not a static faith, but one that grows. It may start like a mustard seed, but it continues to grow in knowledge, revelation, power and influence as one follows the injunction of Jude to build up ourselves on our Most Holy Faith.

It is a faith that produces proofs and tangible results and transforming influence in human life irrespective of race, culture, class or gender. It is available to all anytime, anywhere and anyhow. All that is needed is a simple acceptance and belief in the truth of God's love reaching out to us, like the Father of the prodigal son, irrespective of where we are currently. This faith is an active faith that dynamically causes effects and reactions in people, places or things and circumstances.

This faith we proclaim has evidence. There's evidence in Jerusalem, go there. There's evidence in archeology, through which they have found many thing's that the bible recorded. The bible already said the world was round, because God *sits upon the circle of the earth*" (Isaiah

40:22), even before Pythagoras said it, and Columbus proved it through sailing.

When NASA found a day missing in the world's calendar, they could not find the answer in any physics, mathematical, or scientific journals. They found the answer in the Bible, in Joshua 10:12 when Joshua told the sun and the moon to stand still for about a day. They calculated that to be 23 hours and 20 minutes. So they said okay, but we still have 40 minutes missing. So where is the missing 40 minutes? No book could answer it. But the bible answered it. Because there is a king called Hezekiah in 2 Kings 20:1-11 who God sent his prophet, Isaiah to and said:

"...Set thine house in order; for thou shalt die, and not live." (2 Kings 20:1).

The bible further tells us that the king immediately turned his face to the wall and pleaded his case with God. And before the prophet could leave the palace, God said to him go back and tell him I give him fifteen more years". Hezekiah asked,

"...What shall be the sign that the LORD will heal me," (v8)

Isaiah responded saying

"...shall the shadow go forward ten degrees, or go back ten degrees?" (v9).

Hezekiah requested that it is easier for ten degrees to go forward in the Sun Dial of Ahaz, but it would rather be a miracle for it to go backward ten degrees. And God turned the clock (the Sun Dial of Ahaz) backwards 10 degrees. If you know your geography very well, you will know that longitudinally, every longitude is 4 minutes. So 4 multiplied by 10 is equal to 40 minutes. So NASA proved the missing day from the bible by adding the 23 hours 20 minutes of Joshua to the 40 minutes of Hezekiah's request and they got 24 hours - a day!

There are many prophecies in the bible that have been fulfilled in the last one hundred years. The most significant for me, is the case of the nation of Israel. In Zechariah 8:7-8, the bible records:

"Thus saith the LORD of hosts; Behold, I will save my people from the east country, and from the west country;

And I will bring them, and they shall dwell in the midst of Jerusalem: and they shall be my people, and I will be their God, in truth and in righteousness".

For those who were Christians in 1946/47, this was still a prophecy expected to be fulfilled. That changed on May 14, 1948 when Israel was established and declared as a Jewish state. This was subsequent to the adoption of resolution 181(ii) by the general assembly of the United Nations on November 29, 1947. Until 1948, there was no nation called Israel as we know it today. Israel as a people was scattered from the first century, and the Jews were all over the world without any country of their own from the 1st century until 1948. God said to them "*I will scatter you among the nations...*" (Leviticus 26:33) and He did exactly as He had said. He scattered the Jews from 100AD to 1948AD. The planting of Israel as a nation is an indictment on every person alive today who calls himself or herself an atheist, who says I don't believe in God. The bible, to start with, says:

"The fool says in his heart, there's no God...." (Psalm 14:1)

Only a fool will say there is no God. When He gave them their land as He promised, the Jews although a small people group with a population of about 9 million people have produced the highest number of Nobel Laureates in the world. It is important to note that the events that preceded the establishment of Israel as a nation in 1948, and thereafter are just not natural ones. Do you know that if you remove everything Israel has invented to date as we know it, life will grind to a halt?

To start with, imagine today the convenience of having your cell phone? Technologies developed in Israel play a very significant part in every cell phone used worldwide. If you say you don't believe in God, tell me how a nation of nine million people can have such significant influence on the global economy. Unless there is a sovereign God, who fulfills covenant is with them, how could this be? Unless there is a God of Abraham, the God of Isaac and the God of Jacob, who is moving and working through them, how could they have achieved all these?

There is a God in heaven directing their affairs. If you think God is not God, Israel as a nation is the proof. For a nation that started to exist in 1948 to control the economy of the world, is not possible naturally, it is God at work. What you have just read now should make you so happy you're a Christian. This is because God keeps His covenants. You may break your own, but God will keep His. The Covenant with Abraham is in perpetuity, it cannot be broken. It doesn't mean they will go to Heaven, and that's why we preach to the Jew's to get saved.

In summary, our faith is not stagnant, it grows, active, enduring and cannot fail, it produces proofs and tangible results and it has transforming influence. Jesus said in Matthew 17:20 that if your faith be like a grain of mustard seed, that is not visible to the eyes, it would eventually become a big tree. That is why you shouldn't underestimate the grace of God on your life. Our most Holy faith is not an optional life. It is the only life that should be lived. It is the only life that God approves of. Jesus Christ said:

"I am the way, the truth and the life, no man comes to the Father, except by me." (John 14:6)

It is an enduring faith that cannot fail. It is not a faith that leads to bondage, but a liberating one that cannot be defeated. It is a winning and an overcoming faith, and it represents the totality of what the Christian is and believes. It is not a religion and not a way of life. It is the life of the Christian. As dogmatic as this may sound, the Lord Jesus

Christ legally earned this position, because He is the ONLY Propitiation for our sin. He was the only one who died for our sins as a substitute, and was validated by God who raised Him from the dead. He thus would be the only one qualified to judge all men based on whether they accept and believe in His sacrificial death and receive the gift of eternal life (John 3:16-17 and Acts 17:30-31).

CHAPTER 2

The Just Shall Live By Faith – Foundational Principles of Faith

Once we come into this most Holy faith, it is important to understand that our faith is not static and does not just end with becoming a believer. The ensuing life we live must and has to be a life of faith. The life we now live as believers and disciples of the Lord Jesus Christ must imperatively be *a life of faith and lived in faith.*

In the previous chapter, it was said that our faith is in the existence of the Triune God, God the father, God the son and God the Holy Spirit. It was further said that our faith is rooted and founded on the word of God. This faith is resolutely based on the tangibility and reality of God. You are not just a Christian for one year, or a few years, but with an eternal perspective and holding on to the end. It continues into the life after.

Furthermore, this faith works by love and partners with God. It is an audacious and confident faith. Indeed, it is our most Holy faith. Our faith is not static, but continues to grow. It can mature, and can be stronger. It may start like a grain of mustard seed and can grow to become a mighty tree. Our faith produces proof and tangible results that. transform lives. Our faith is not optional, and everyone is commanded to repent – Acts 17:30-31, why? It is because in verse 31 we read that,

"God has appointed a day, in which he's going to judge the world by that one man, who he has ordained..."

That one man is the Lord Jesus Christ, and to prove that He's going to do that; He raised Him from the dead. Jesus is alive. He is risen and He's not in the grave. So our faith is predicated on, and our reliance is built on Jesus. No Jesus no Christian faith. You must never be confused about who Jesus is. You must know Him for yourself and have a relationship with Him. The only life to be lived on this earth is the Christian life - the life of Jesus. In 2 Corinthians 5:15 we are told, if you are living at all, you should live unto Jesus, because He died for you.

"And that he died for all, that they which live should not henceforth live unto themselves, but unto him which died for them, and rose again." (2 Corinthians 5:15)

Do you know you have no right to live for yourself? This is what I want you to work on as you work out your salvation with fear and trembling.

THE JUST SHALL LIVE BY FAITH.

In this chapter, I want us to examine the phrase **"...the just shall live by faith..."**. What does that mean? This scripture phrase occurs four times in the bible. When God says something twice you should pay attention, thrice, you should pay close attention, and the fourth time you better read it carefully. This scripture was the reason why Martin Luther, the theologian and reformer (1483 – 1546) could single handedly stand up against the then established Church. This one scripture changed Martin Luther's life. He refused to accept the decadence of the church in his days. He declared to them, what you are practicing is not the bible and he stood up and said "No, salvation cannot be bought, the just shall live by faith"

One man, because of his conviction based on the word of God, changed the world. This Martin Luther who lived in the 15-16th century inspired the reformation, because the church at that time was away from God. He insisted that the just shall live by faith and salvation is by faith, not by buying it with money. Why is this scripture important? It is the foundation for our Christian faith. A Christian will not be one without faith. We are saved by grace through faith.

"For by grace are ye saved through faith; and that not of yourselves: it is the gift of God: Not of works, lest any man should boast." (Ephesians 2:8-9).

This simply means if you don't put your faith in Jesus, you can't be born again. So to be born again, you lean on/put your faith in Jesus. In Ephesians 2:8 we learnt that we are saved by grace through the agency of faith. In Romans 5:1 the bible also says *"… being justified by faith, we have peace with God."* Being justified by faith means just as if you never sinned. It means that when God looks at your record now, it is clean. That is what it means to be born again.

Like the thief on the cross. Jesus said today you will be with me in paradise (Luke 23:43). How did that happen? Right there because he had faith in Jesus, and he received justification. Justification means, you are discharged and acquitted of guilt. That means although last night, you were a criminal, yet because you put your faith in Jesus today, and you say Lord I accept you as my Lord and Savior, your slate is wiped clean. Please understand that as a Christian, that the day you got born again, the sins you committed twenty, ten, and five years ago, and the sin you inherited from Adam have all been forgiven and forgotten because you were justified. By faith we are saved, by faith we are justified, and *"the just shall live by faith."* *In a nutshell, we are saved by faith, we are justified by faith, and we are to live by faith.*

Who is this just person? The just is a sinner made righteous. It is a state of being right with God, and you are in perfect agreement with Him. So there is neither difference nor barrier between you and God. It means you are at peace with God, and your sins are forgiven. You are His child, and He is now your father. God is committed to you, you are committed to Him, and therefore your works should now be patterned after who you are. A fish swims and not fly, birds fly and not swim, likewise a justified person therefore must behave like God.

If you say you are born again of the spirit of God, you have no other way to live, but by faith. For example, if you take the fish out of the water, it will die, if you take a Christian out of faith, she/he will die spiritually. A Christian must live and walk by faith. That is what this scripture is saying. The first time it occurred in the bible is in Habakkuk 2:4:

"Behold his soul which is lifted up is not upright in him: but the just shall live by his faith."

Habakkuk is talking about pride here, and then he puts that conjunction "*but*". Anytime you see that word "*but*" in the bible pay close attention, and it is very important to note what comes thereafter. "**But**" is a conjunction, and it's like when you are driving and you get to a corner you slow down. So anytime you see "*but*" in the bible, wait for what's next.

So Habakkuk says "*...but the just shall live by his faith.*" Now this is the only word in the Old Testament from the original Hebrew, and that word "*just*", means somebody who is in perfect agreement with the commandment of God. It is because at that time, Jesus had not come, and God had to make provision for justification. So who was just in the Old Testament? Anyone who did (obeyed) the word of God was considered just. It did not mean they were perfect, but as long as they obeyed the voice of God and did what God wanted them to do, they were just before Him. For example, Abraham, David and Elijah were justified before God, but were they perfect? No! But they were 'Just', because they agreed with the commandments of God and they lived by their faith in God. Romans 4:3 reveals to us how Abraham's faith became the yardstick for his justification by God: *"Abraham believed God and it was counted unto him for righteousness."* (Romans 4:3).

So if you look at Abraham, or David, they both acted in faith. In contrast, Israel looked at Goliath and they chickened out. Some Christians also easily give up even today. They run away from the problems of the world, and run to hide in a safe place. They don't want to attend to problems and become solution providers, but not David who had faith in God. He looked at Goliath and said, "Who is this uncircumcised philistine? I am going to take him out." What was the propelling force behind David? His faith in God. The others wouldn't believe, but he chose to believe. So we see here that in the Old Testament the justified ones lived by their faith, confirming the words of Habakkuk "*...the Just shall live by HIS FAITH.*"

This also brings out the fact that Faith is personal (It will be discussed in detail in Chapter 4). It doesn't matter who you are as long as you live by your faith, and it can get you to places beyond your wildest imagination. The second time this phrase is repeated in the Bible is in Romans 1:17.

"For therein is the righteousness of God revealed from faith to faith: as it is written, the just shall live by faith."

There is a lot to learn in this passage, but primarily it teaches us that faith is progressive. You don't have to remain where you are, your faith can grow. You can become stronger, just like when you go to the gym, you put on more muscles, and you can lift more weights. That is the way faith is. Faith actually is like a muscle. You can exercise your faith, and when you do, you get stronger, and your spiritual muscle grows stronger. That's what Paul was saying here, which is that in the righteousness of God your faith can grow from one level to another, from the beginning to the end, from initial start/immaturity to perfection/maturity.

The more you practice living by faith, the more your faith will grow and mature. In the same verse Paul said "*as it is written*". You have to know that it is written. God is not going to change that. He chided the Galatians about their drawing back from their faith in the Lord Jesus Christ, and trying to relapse to the law, and argued vehemently that justification does not come by the law, but by faith as we read in Galatians 3:11:

"But that no man is justified by the law in the sight of God, it is evident: for, the just shall live by faith".

This verse now makes it the third time the phrase being discussed occurred in the Bible, and the continuous reference to it signifies its importance. The explicit focus on this verse under review is the superiority of the dispensation of grace over that of the law. Paul was emphatic about the fact that now in the new dispensation; justification could no longer be by human performance of the works of the law, but by faith in the finished work of the Lord Jesus Christ. This justification marks the beginning of the "just" (believer) living by faith. In Hebrews 10:38 we see the phrase repeated the fourth and last time:

"Now the just shall live by faith: but if any man draw back, my soul shall have no pleasure in him."

This time however, Paul added a very important phrase *"...but if any man draw back..."* May you not fall by the way side. Let me encourage you, even if a Christian falls, it is not the end of the person and that is how powerful our faith is. Even if the enemy gives you a technical knockout, and you were counted out, don't give up. You may be down, but not knocked out because Job 14:7 says:

"For there is hope of a tree, if it be cut down, that it will sprout again, and that the tender branch thereof will not cease."

No matter how bad the enemy knocked you down and says you are finished, you are not finished because all you just need are the scents of the word of God, power of prayer and the anointing and something glorious will begin to happen to you again. As long as you, justified man or woman, continue to live by faith you cannot be defeated. You will have battles, you'll fight, there will be challenges in life, but you'll always win because the just shall live by faith.

You have to live by faith, and not by what you hear, see or feel. You must have faith in God, and not the economy or government. You are to pray for the government and not to put your faith in them. The government cannot really help you. Have faith in Him who created the nation. There is a power above all powers, there is a God called the God of the nations, He rules in the affairs of men. God can change the laws of this country to change your life. The God whom the bible says upholds the world by the word of His power. Do you know that God suspends the world by His word? God, Jehovah is holding the planet earth in space, by His word. And sometimes when He just wants to relax, the bible says "**the earth is his foot stool**" (Matthew 5:35, Acts 7:49, Isaiah 66:1).

Do you know that according to Isaiah 40:15 the whole world or planet earth is in the negative? The biggest respect that God gave the world is that you are like a drop in the bucket. In fact, you are nothing. Isaiah went on to say you are less than nothing. And you want to put your faith on the planet earth that God says it is my footstool? Have faith in God because the just shall live by faith.

If the Christian has no option but to live by faith, then what is faith? The word faith comes from the Greek word "PISTIS"; it simply means strong conviction, not a weak one. Faith is not presumption, guess work, or an assumption. Faith is strong conviction based on knowledge and revelation of the truth. Faith is a firm conviction that produces a full, complete, total acknowledgement of God's revelation and truth. Faith is conviction based on what you have heard. What have you heard? And what are you convinced about? Are you convinced about God? Do you really believe in God? This is faith itemized in a nutshell:

1. You believe there's a God.
2. You believe in what He said.
3. You are convinced about what He said.

Let me give you an example, Abraham, take your son Isaac, go and sacrifice him. Do you ever hear of any argument between Abraham and God? The bible says the following day, Abraham took his son and was going to sacrifice him, and when they got to the mountain, Abraham really was going to do it, why?

1. Abraham believed God, he trusted God.
2. He knew that it was God that spoke, not a demon, a devil, his wife, or somebody else.

He knew that the voice he heard was God's. He heard the voice of God, God cannot lie and God is not a man, God cannot cheat you, God does not hate you, and God does not wish you evil. So he believed in God, he believed His word, and he was convinced. He did not even discuss with Sarah that he was going ahead to sacrifice Isaac. That is faith. If we treat God that way, our lives will change.

So faith begins by believing in God. You have to know that this God is not your pastor; He is not a human being. Faith is not what my friend told me, or what is happening in the church, but who I believe God is, because sometimes man can be wrong. Your friends can be so wrong, people around you can be so wrong, so your faith cannot be in man, otherwise it will fail. Your faith must be in God. Our faith must not be in the wrong place.

If your faith is in the beauty of the city where you live, what happens if a tornado strikes and the whole city is wiped out, what are you going to do? God forbid, because it has happened in this country a whole city was wiped out by tornado. You want to tell me all of them were sinners? There were Christians there. What would you do? You are in New Jersey; the house you are living in for forty years is gone. What is going to happen to you? If all your faith was in the house you inherited from your grandfather, but it's gone now, what are you going to do?

No matter how rich, poor, or educated you are, you must live by your faith. Learn never to put your faith in things that perish, because they are temporary. One of the things we put faith in, is money. You know the bible says money has wings. Money can fly, but what you want is faith in God, because God can decide to fly money from Australia, London or South Africa to you. As long as you have faith in God, God can do anything. The just shall live by faith.

"Faith is the substance of things we hope for, the evidence of things we do not see" (Hebrews 11:1).

What does the word substance mean? It is a legal term, and it means a title deed, or a guarantee. When you buy a house, the only legal evidence of your purchase to show that you own the house is the title deed. The title will have Mr. BJ, owner of Lot A, Block C, Dallas City addition, title deed, and that is valid anywhere, and no attorney, no president, and no judge can argue about it. This is because on the day you close on your house, you signed and the title deed was issued in your name.

This explanation confirms why your faith is very important. You cannot lay claim to anything that you do not have its title deed. Faith is the title deed of what you are hoping for. It is the title deed, or legal document to support what you are believing God for.

But somebody may say where is the legal document? In God's undiluted word the example of the legal document is: *"…by his stripes you are healed."* (Isaiah 53:5)

Or *"with the heart, man believes, and with the mouth confession is made into salvation."* (Romans 10:10)

Or *"I wish above all things that thou may prosper and be in health even as your soul prospers"* (3 John 2) etc.

So at the low level, faith is the word of God, or it is the substance of things hoped for. We are expecting the evidence, the proof of the things we have not yet seen.

For example, God told Abraham, you are going to have a son. So what was his substance or his title deed? It was the word of God. Just because you doubt does not mean you have lost faith. True faith will face test. Abraham believed when God told him you are going to have a son, but somewhere along the line Sarah said "Abraham, I think God is delaying, I think we can help Him. Can you try Hagar and see whether this will work?" Don't ever try to help God. If you hold on, your change will come (Job 14:14). Abraham heard God say to him, you will have a son, and that was the substance, the title deed, or the legal document. That is why Romans 10:17 says:

"So then faith cometh by hearing, and hearing by the word of God."

So Abraham believed and received his title deed. Faith was the substance (or title deed) of the son he hoped for. What is the evidence? The word of God, the assurance that if God said it, I believe it and that settles it.

One of the key issues about faith is that we like to talk to God, but we don't want to wait to hear from Him. You need to hear from God. Sometimes you are praying about something, God will tell you "Don't worry it is done". Once upon a time God told me saying "Hold your peace; don't worry" This was because I was worried. Your being alive today is an evidence that when God says it, He will do it. God said thank me. In the natural I could not thank God. But God said "Thank me" God said "dance". So I danced in my car because my heart was heavy. So my dancing became faith that is the substance, the title deed of what I am hoping for, and it is the only evidence I have of what I have not yet seen.

If God promised you a baby, you will have a baby. Faith is the conviction that we have what we don't yet see. That is why the bible says in Romans

4:20 that Abraham staggered not in faith, he was neither worried nor moved, but he kept believing until Sarah brought forth a son. Faith is a force that produces results. Faith is based on the word of God, so the just shall live by faith. The word 'live' talks about the period you are going to be alive on this earth as a Christian, and you have to live by faith.

If you are not a Christian, the faith you need is to be born again or get saved. That's where you begin, believe and make peace with God, receive the forgiveness of your sins and become a child of God. All you need to do is believe that Jesus died for your sins, believe that God will forgive you if you confess and forsake you sins, you will have eternal life. That is what you need to become a Christian. Now that you are a Christian, for the remaining span of your life on earth, what the bible is saying is this; you have to live by faith.

The word "live" means your daily life style, your walk with God, your conduct, and day to day living. So let's illustrate, you wake up in the morning, the weather is very bad, you now say "Oh what a terrible day" don't ever say that. Say "Hallelujah, blessed be the name of the Lord, it is a great day. Amen, it shall be well with me today, I am blessed and highly favored." So you wake up in the morning, sometimes you feel tired, don't worry, but get up slowly. Don't jump out of bed. Take it slowly. So when you wake up say "Thank God for this day".

By the time you dress up and you remember I have not paid the electric bill, water bill, insurance etc. just say by faith "Okay, it is well in Jesus name." Take your mind off it, and don't worry. Then do the next reasonable thing, pray and say, "I pray that my bills will be paid in Jesus name, amen." Now, they haven't been paid yet but start to say it. "My bills will be paid." Then you remember that your aunty has cancer, you say "Cancer you go in Jesus name." You begin to believe what you want. Don't say "How will I pay this bill O God?" Because of the pressure, if you are not careful, before you know it you will have heart attack.

The devil is a liar. Don't focus on the problems but on God. Focus on God, and on His word. So your life style must match that of Christ. No matter your situation, when you wake up in the morning, adopt the right attitude. Don't allow the devil to intimidate you.

You are calling those things that be not as though they were when you begin to speak to your circumstance, and you begin to read the word of God. If it is sickness, go to healing scriptures, if you need finances, go to the word of God and it will tell you, pay your tithe, and honor God with your substance and He will fill your barns with plenty. It is all there in Proverbs 3. So you take those scriptures and say, "Lord I am honoring you, Lord help me, I can't lose my job, I am a tithe payer." Why? Your title deed is the word of God.

Many times I need God to show up for me, I say God, I pay my tithe, you have to bless me. Your word says when I pay my tithe; you will open the windows of heaven and pour out a blessing on me. I believe your word, and the scriptures cannot be broken. That is faith. So every part of your life is all about faith and you must learn how to engage a husband by faith, get a wife by faith, and get a job or promotion by faith.

For example, many years ago, as a contractor I accidentally saw that a colleague was making more money than I. I said "What? We are doing the same job and were given different pay rate?" So I got to my table and I sent an email to the recruiter, telling her I want you to increase my hourly rate by $10 dollars now. The recruiter replied back and said okay we will see. Within a few days she said yes. With hindsight I would have requested for $20, and they would have given me.

Brethren, everything hinges on faith, everything. When I was looking for a wife, I used to worry a lot when I was about twenty-one years old. One day in my quiet time God said "Go to psalm 16 and I read Psalm 16 and it says:

"The lines are fallen unto me in pleasant places; yea, I have a goodly heritage."

In the natural, I had nobody, so from that day, I relaxed. God said to me, "it's going to be well".

The day I proposed to my wife to be, Anne, I got a yes on the spot and we had dinner. The just shall live by faith... everything in the kingdom is by faith. While I was a student during my senior year in college, I woke up one morning, opened my textbook, and I saw a question and the Holy Spirit witnessed to my spirit that "This question is coming out tomorrow." So I went next door to my colleague, I said open that book, that question is coming out tomorrow". When we got to the exam hall, the question from the book came out word for word. Like John said, I am not talking to you what I have read in the bible, I am talking to you about what my hands have touched, what my eyes have seen, and what I have experienced.

So in every area of your life you must live by faith, because this is where many Christians fall short. For example, with regards to your money, you must give an offering by faith. This is because sometimes, all you have is $100 and the Holy Spirit may say give all you have. You better give it because when God sent Elijah to the widow of Zarephath, Elijah said to her "Give me water to drink", but as the lady was going, Elijah said "No, come back, give me lunch." The woman said. "Ah man of God. I only have one lunch left to eat with my son and die". Elijah said, "Give it to me". If it is today some of you will curse Elijah out saying "Look at this wicked Pastor, he calls himself a man of God, and he is asking for my last meal, and he wants to eat it."

Faith sometimes and in most cases does not make sense. This is where many of us miss it. Many of us are going to be in situations where God is going to test us. **You don't graduate (mature) in the kingdom of God except through test.** It does not make sense to give your last meal to a prophet, and many of us missed it that way. This is the key. God wanted to bless the woman. The woman did not know that when God wants to bless you, He will send you somebody. The woman gave Elijah food, and for the rest of her life, she had food. She had no lack. Faith doesn't make sense, yet this woman obeyed. Praise the Lord!

The just living by faith is the foundational principle of the life of faith, God expects the believer to live. We must be assured of our salvation and justification with God. Deuteronomy 8:3 and Matthew 4:4 teach us that "…man does not and should not live by natural bread alone, but by every word that proceeds from the mouth of God…" God expects us to conduct our lives by the dictates of the word of God. We see that the Lord Jesus Christ as a man on the earth never did anything of His own accord (John 5:30). Everything He did from His baptism and commissioning to His temptation, ministry activities and eventual death on the cross were all in line and fulfillment of the scriptures.

As a believer, Paul eloquently shows in Galatians 2:20, that we are crucified with Christ: nevertheless, we live, yet not us living, but Christ who lives in us: and the life which we now live in the flesh we live by the faith of Christ who loved us and gave Himself for us. Thus the faith we live by as believers and disciples is the overcoming faith of Christ in us.

Thus we should learn to believe and do the word of God, obey it and trust Him. The end result is to cultivate a lifestyle of living our lives through the lens/mirror of the word of God. ***For the word we know, experience and practice, is what we become.*** Hence faith which comes by hearing the word of God would continue to grow in us as we consistently live victorious lives. I pray that you will learn to live by faith and prove God's faithfulness in your life. AMEN.

CHAPTER 3

The Purpose of Faith

We learnt extensively in the earlier chapter that the just shall live by faith, and as mentioned earlier, it means if you're a Christian, the only way to live is to live by faith. Many of us sometimes live by other ways, and neither by faith, nor by trust in God. We live by what our friends advise us, and we forget Psalm 1:1 that says:

"Blessed is the man that walketh not in the counsel of the ungodly, nor standeth in the way of sinners, nor sitteth in the seat of the scornful..."

When the bible says that "*...the Just shall live by faith*" it simply means you can't live by your senses, that is, by what you see, hear or feel. You have to live by faith. This chapter aims to address the rationale and purpose for living by faith. Let us briefly examine them below.

1) **If you don't live by faith you cannot please God**. (Hebrews 11:6). As a child of God, your first objective is to please God, and not to be a 'man pleaser'. This is the reason your friends sometimes will not like what you do; because it looks foolish to them. When I had to resign my job in England to come to the United States of America, I didn't tell my friends, because they would have told me, you must be crazy. This was because a week after I resigned my job I was granted tenure. That decision to a logical person was foolishness by all natural means, and to crown it all I had no Job waiting for me in the United States of America.

How do you resign your job as a college professor in England and come to the U.S. without a job, you must be crazy? To push the foolishness so-to-speak further, I had no resident permit here, and that's why faith in the natural has some elements of risk. Faith is not presumption. Please if you have not heard from God, don't take a step. Don't marry that man unless you have an assurance or clear guidance from God for real. Don't go into that business unless you are really led of God. But if God speaks, He will move on your behalf. When you know His voice, you move. You do his will. So why do you have to exercise faith? Hebrews 11:6 says:

"But without faith, it is impossible to please God. For he that comes to God must believe..."

You must believe in His word, that there is a God. You must believe God is a person, He is real, and is tangible. He is also a person who has eyes, ears, hands, and legs and He speaks. God has feelings, and He can be hurt. Even though He is a person, yet He is God and not a man. So don't confuse Him with humans. The bible says in Psalm 90:2 *"...from everlasting to everlasting, thou art God."* So don't try to reason Him out. Your brain does not have the capacity to understand the totality of who He is.

I am a very cerebral and logical person. I reason things out. However, when I am in the church or dealing with God, I submit my human intelligence to Gods' word, knowing that it is limited when dealing with a supernatural God. I thank God for that grace and ability yet I can transition between both worlds. If I am in the classroom I lecture engineering for three hours, but when I am in church, I know there are some things in God that engineering cannot explain.

In fact, in mathematics, what I said earlier is - from minus infinity to plus infinity. Go and ask any mathematician, no one can tell you or fully explain what infinity is. Go and check it. In mathematics, there is a sign, infinity, or more generally negative infinity and positive infinity.

Negative Infinity is like no beginning; Positive infinity is like no ending. Infinity is akin to God that has no limits, who cannot be defined or contained. FROM everlasting (minus infinity) TO Everlasting (plus infinity), thou art God – (Psalm 90:2).

So without faith it is impossible to please God. If you want God to be happy with you, believe/trust Him. Believe what the bible says because it is true. People can be wrong unless they're speaking what agrees with the bible. Any word that is contrary to the bible is a lie. So without faith, it is impossible to please God, for he that cometh to God must believe that God is. We please God by giving due attention to His word and obeying His word as we exercise our faith in Him.

2) **God rewards those who diligently seek him.** God rewards those who hunger after Him. My challenge to you this day is, be a God chaser. The purpose of exercising your faith is to please Him, and that is the only way you can please Him. God responds to faith, when you believe Him, He will move on your behalf.

Why must I believe God? For example, it is impossible for a woman without a womb to have a child, but not with God: "*...for with God all things are possible.*" (Mark 10:27) With man, it is impossible for one stone to kill a giant, but not with God. With man, it is impossible to cross the Red Sea or for the sea to part for you, but not with God. With man it is impossible to get a job that you don't qualify for, but not with God. But with God, all things are possible. With man, it is not possible for you to move from prison and become the Prime Minister of a country. This was the case with Joseph.

Brethren, God can change the weather pattern for you. God can change the government in one day. Communism collapsed before my eyes in one day. I saw it, and I'll never forget that day in London, England watching it on live television. When communism began to crumble, the Romanian Prime Minister who was one of the anchors of communism, knowing his game was up, ran out of his house to the roof, boarded a helicopter and escaped for his life. Here was a man who everyone feared in the country, but when the structure that brought him to power, and sustained him there collapsed, he knew the wisest thing for him to do at that time was to run away. That was the day Berlin wall also came down. God in one fell swoop ended communism.

Some people may never understand because they have no clue about some of the prayers we used to pray in the late 70's and early 80's. The night vigils we used to have back home in Africa, for communism to collapse. So it is one of my greatest testimonies I am going to take to heaven because I lived and prayed to see the collapse of communism. We always prayed for the Christians that were persecuted in the Eastern Block, we used to wail in Africa, and cry to God, "O God bring down communism." It is incumbent on the church today to continue to intercede and bind the evil spirit behind communism. I lived to see it happen because with man it was impossible, but with God, all things are possible. That is why we believe Him. With God, anything is possible. With God, fire can become a refrigerator. With God, a lion can become your pillow just like Daniel did. Snake can roll on your hand, you'd shake it off into the fire and nothing will happen to you like Paul. With God, all things are possible.

Why must you have faith in God? It is because God has put in you the ability to change your world. Jesus speaking again in Mark 9:23 lays the action of faith at the feet of man saying "*...if thou canst believe, all things are possible to him that believeth.*" The problem obviously is not with God. Often times as Christians until we are desperate, we don't really see the manifestation of God. Sometimes God will force you to desperation like He did to Joshua. When he was in the battle against the Amorites, no one ever told Joshua he could command the sun and moon to stand still till he finished prosecuting the battle. And the bible tells us in Joshua 10:14: "*And there was no day like that before it or after it, that the LORD hearkened unto the voice of a man: for the LORD fought for Israel.*"

It is the only one time that it happened in the bible, none before then, nor after then that God hearkened to the voice of man who acted in unusual faith. A man commanded the sun to be stationary. The Lord Jesus said, "*if thou canst believe,*" If you can believe the cripple will walk. If you can believe, the dead will be raised. God is able to do what He said he would do. That's why Paul said why do you find it inconceivable that God can raise the dead (Acts 26:8). God has raised the dead in many parts of the world, and that's the worst thing that can happen to man. To me that's the greatest miracle - that somebody can die and come back to life. But God has done it worldwide.

A nurse in Latin America was reported to have raised two dead people. She's not a preacher, but a regular believer. So you have no excuse. She's a nurse and she read that scripture, she believed it, and God has used her to raise two dead people. You have not seen God face to face, believe Him, that's why it's called faith. For faith is the substance of things we hope for, the evidence, and the proof of what I haven't yet seen. So faith is that, I believe God and then I will see. And that is how the kingdom of God operates.

In the natural kingdom you have to see to believe. God does not operate that way. You have to believe, and then you see. The day Pastor Anne and myself came in front of our church building, there were three families meeting in our house. When we got there, she said you must be joking. Are you really thinking of this place? The building looked massive and intimidating, yet I told her let's take the first step make a phone call.

See there are things we can do. I have faith, she has action. So I said, make the phone call. I saw the place, I believed. In the natural it does not make sense. There were just three families meeting in our house, and we came to the front of the massive building, which is now our church building, and I said God is sending me there? Those who knew our membership and the size of the building would say "You must be crazy." But there was fire of conviction in my spirit. I said to her, "Let me tell you why. When I knew about this place I began to dream again. I began to see things in the spirit that God could do." That was what provided the faith to believe.

May God cause you to see what you have not yet seen. May you be like Abraham who staggered, not in faith but believed God and said I know I am 95 years old, I will have a son. May God cause you to see. That's why God said "*Abraham, look at the stars, and the sand upon the sea shore.*" God will always give you a dream to propel your faith.

If thou canst believe, all things are possible. If you can believe, God can open the wall for you, shut the mouth of lions, and give you a Boaz as a husband even though you are a foreigner to the commonwealth of Israel. If you can believe like Esther, you can become the queen. Anything is possible with God.

3) **We see another purpose for living by faith in God.** In Hebrews 4:2, Paul writes that:

"*For unto us was the gospel preached, as well as unto them: but the word preached did not profit them, not being mixed with faith in them that heard it.*"

The preaching of the word the Israelites heard did not profit or benefit them because it was not mixed with faith. They did not believe God. So Paul, writing in Hebrews was warning us, don't be like the Israelites who did not trust God whole heartedly. As long as you're living in this world; you have to live by faith. Don't let what you see move you. What are you believing God for? Continue to believe God until you see your change come (Job 14:14). The purpose of Faith therefore is to enable you to profit in this life from the blessings and favor of God and to live a victorious life.

God desires that as long as you live in this world, you will profit in your life. That word profit there is not just talking about money alone.

It actually means that God wants His word to benefit you in every area of your life. He wants you to profit in your marriage, health, job, and business. You must profit in life, in the works of your hand, and ministry. The will of God is that every believer should be successful, but the only way that can happen is for you to believe what you hear, the word of God you read, and by mixing (uniting) it with faith. Until you mix/unite the word you hear with faith, it does not do you any good.

It is not enough to hear. Romans 10 says "*…. faith comes by hearing, and hearing by the word of God.*" Release your faith, and believe God. What is the purpose of faith? It is available to us so that we can profit in life, and live through life successfully. Why is that so? It is because in life, you're going to face problems and oppositions but the bible says,

"Many are the afflictions of the righteous." (Psalm 34:19)

So stop complaining and face the facts because in this life, you're going to face challenges (John 16:33). That is just what life is all about. Even though the afflictions of the righteous are many, yet "*…the Lord delivers him out of them all.*" Blessed be the name of the Lord, who is our very present help in the time of trouble.

Challenges of life prepare us for maturity. You cannot be a solid Christian when you have not fought battles. You don't just wake up one day and suddenly claim to be a four-star General. You have to fight battles. How many battles have you fought? How many enemies have you defeated? There are different categories of battles - some battles are meant for four star generals, some for corporals, sergeants, or recruits. God is good and He does not allow you to confront battles that are bigger than your capacity. He would not allow a battle meant for a four-star general to be placed before you, a recruit. He will never do it because:

"…God is faithful, who will not suffer you to be tempted above that ye are able; but will with the temptation also make a way to escape, that ye may be able to bear it." – 1 Corinthians 10:13.

Bend your knees and pray, cry to God, call upon God, because when God gives you victory it promotes you in the kingdom, and it begins to give you an audacity. I have seen God move, and I don't doubt this God. That is why I always pay my tithe, because I have tasted His hand of promotion in my life. I know this God can change the laws because of me. Faith is to profit you so that when you face a problem in life, you don't need to be afraid. All you need to do is rise up, and say no to the devil - bring it on. Let me show you in Psalm 27:1 a principle of faith.

"The Lord is my light and my salvation, whom shall I fear?"

That is level one, or first grade. That means you know that God is your light, you know He is your salvation, fear not because there are 365 fear nots in the bible. Meaning everyday there is a fear not. In continuing the verse David said *"...whom shall I fear?"* And concluding verse 1 he said,

"The Lord is the strength of my life of whom shall I be afraid?"

When you start getting promotion you start attracting haters. Don't worry about them, they are the ones referred to in verse 2:

"When the wicked, even mine enemies and my foes, came upon me to eat up my flesh, they stumbled and fell."

Those evil ones when they come to try to eat up your flesh, talk about you, try to destroy your credibility, become your adversaries and your foes, they will stumble, and fall.

Now, because you are winning battles, because of God's help in verse 2 you have to be anointed enough because people are going to throw mud at you. They will gossip about you, and call you names. But you have to have sufficient grace to withstand them when they throw mud at you, and you keep moving the mud just drops. In the process they will be going backward, while you are moving forward. Because you're a seed of Christ operating in His kingdom, they can neither stop nor limit you. When they come against you, they will stumble and fall.

Once you begin to walk at that level, God will promote you because now you are ready to deal with the adversary, and those who will gang up against you. The Psalmist says in verse 3 *"...though a host should encamp against me, my heart shall not fear:"*. The last part of this verse is advanced level and David said *".... though war should rise against me, in this will I be confident."* Even if the whole country, should rise against me, in this will I be confident. A Christian is most dangerous when you back him or her against the wall. That is the prayer I pray for you that may God make you desperate enough, so that you have nowhere else to go.

It means Egypt is chasing you behind and you cannot go back, the mountain is on the left, you cannot go left, the mountain is on your right, you cannot go right, and before you is the Red sea. May you have a red sea to cross by faith to get to your Canaan; otherwise, you'll die in the wilderness. But you will not die. That's what David was saying here. When a host comes against me, bring it on because like an eagle I don't run from the storm. Let me tell you, what separates the eagle from other birds. It is because it is uniquely endowed, and it's the only bird God compares Himself and Christians with.

When there's a storm, the eagle starts to look for the worst place in the tornado/storm. The eagle starts spying. Then when the eagle finds the hottest place in the tornado, it focuses on it and watches it. As the storm comes closer, the eagle then spreads its wings and just before it gets to the eagle, the eagle will just lift, and it begins to ride the stormy wind - that's all the eagle does. And that's why the bible says "You soar" as eagle. It does not flap. Lord anoint me not to flap in Jesus name. May God anoint you not to flap (human energy and effort). Problems are supposed to lift you up so that you start to soar like the eagle.

You must have faith so that you can profit in this life and be able to deal with life's problems. You must also have faith because there are possessions in this life that you cannot get unless you believe God and lay claim to them. Every believer has a territory, a blessing or something that God assigned to them. God does not want you to cry every week, and so there must be an answer for you in Jesus name. You must possess your possession, your peace, and your joy. You must also possess your marriage, and your life. Your life will not be degraded because "...*upon mount Zion there is deliverance, there's holiness, and the house of Jacob shall possess their possession*" (Obadiah 17).

This is one reason why you need faith, that is, to possess your possessions that rightly belong to you. For example, in Numbers 13, when Caleb, Joshua and the others were sent to spy the lands, and they came back saying "*Oh Moses, we are done for, we cannot make it...*". The bible says that: "*...and Caleb stilled the people before Moses, and said, let us go up at once, and possess it; for we are well able to overcome it.*" – Numbers 13:30. I know the Promised Land is heaven, that's true; there is a promised land for you here too. There's a place called rest. The bible says "*There remained yet a rest for the people of God.*" (Hebrews 4:9).

There is a place here on earth that you and I must come to; it's the place of possessing our possessions. From verse 5 of Joshua 14, when Joshua began to divide the land, the old man Caleb made some very profound statements: when the children of Judah came unto Joshua in Gilgal, and Caleb the son of Jephunneh, the kenesites said unto him:

"*Then the children of Judah came unto Joshua in Gilgal: and Caleb the son of Jephunneh the Kenezite said unto him, Thou knowest the thing that the LORD said unto Moses the man of God concerning me and thee in Kadeshbarnea.*

Forty years old was I when Moses the servant of the LORD sent me from Kadeshbarnea to espy out the land; and I brought him word again as it was in mine heart."

41

Notice that phrase, "***in my heart***" nevertheless, my brethren that went up with me made the heart of the people melt. But I wholly followed the Lord my God. This is Caleb talking. You'll see where he's going, it is an argument here.

"And Moses sware on that day, saying, Surely the land whereon thy feet have trodden shall be thine inheritance, and thy children's forever, because thou hast wholly followed the LORD my God.

And now, behold, the LORD hath kept me alive, as he said, these forty and five years, even since the LORD spake this word unto Moses, while the children of Israel wandered in the wilderness: and now, lo, I am this day fourscore and five years old. As yet I am as strong this day as I was in the day that Moses sent me:"

He was 85 years old, and he said "Joshua don't look at my age". I am as strong at 85 as I was at 40 and my strength is still with me, even so is my strength now for war. I am 85 years old, I can still fight, and I am strong both to go out and come in. Caleb said in verses 12-13 of Joshua 14:

"Now therefore give me this mountain, whereof the LORD spake in that day; for thou heardest in that day how the Anakims were there, and that the cities were great and fenced: if so be the LORD will be with me, then I shall be able to drive them out, as the LORD said.

And Joshua blessed him, and gave unto Caleb the son of Jephunneh Hebron for an inheritance.

Hebron therefore became the inheritance of Caleb the son of Jephunneh the Kenezite unto this day, because that he wholly followed the LORD God of Israel."

This is a practical example of the fact that when you believe God, there is an inheritance on this earth that belongs to you. The only way to get what you are supposed to get is by faith and by following God whole heartedly in your heart. Wherever the sole of your feet treads upon, God has given it to you for an inheritance. You must inherit the United States of America; it is the will of God. If you find yourself in Australia, or India, God expects you to inherit them because it is the principle of God that as long as you are here on this earth, you must possess your possession. There are territories, there's an inheritance you must possess.

You must continue to believe God. You need faith for salvation, healing, deliverance, to have your needs met, for provision, to be faithful, and to succeed in life. You look at the scriptures and you see faith at work in every body, Abraham, Daniel, David, Joseph, Joshua, Caleb at 85 years old, who took over a whole country as his inheritance. God said to Adam in Genesis 1:27-28 where He made them male and female, He blessed them saying:

"Be fruitful, multiply, replenish, subdue the earth and have dominion..."

Have dominion means you should be an over-comer in every area of your life. You should overcome by the word of God. What is the purpose of faith? It is to please God, exercise your faith and possess your possession in the land. It is also to profit in every area of your life. Your joy and your peace should be to see yourself profit, blessed, successful and prosperous. For God has said:

"Beloved, I wish above all things that thou mayest prosper and be in good health, even as thy soul prospers." – 3 John 2.

CHAPTER 4

The Pronouns of Faith – Faith Is Personal

Faith is personal and understanding this is important for every believer. There is also the corporate aspect of the faith, but I want to really focus on the truth that faith is personal, and addressed here in what I call "the pronouns of faith". Earlier I wrote about the adjective of faith, that is, "The Faith". "Our most Holy Faith" or "The Faith" is also a personal one. Your faith, as mentioned earlier in this book, is a growing and rooted faith. As a Christian, there would be times you are not going to feel good. You are not going to feel you are even a Christian. That is when your faith kicks in to carry you on.

Faith is not a feeling. Faith, we already know is the substance, the title deed, and the legal proof of what you believe in God. Faith is the only evidence you have, even though you don't see anything. So often times as a Christian, you have to understand that you must walk by faith and not by sight, not by feelings, not by what you hear. You have to move by the word of God, because that is certain.

In the previous chapter, we examined what is the purpose of faith? Why must we have faith? Why is it important? In this chapter, I want to focus on the fact that faith is personal. So as a Christian, you must own your faith. You must know how to use your faith. Not just depending on your husband's faith, or your wife's faith. Not even your pastor's faith or that of your friend. It is very common particularly in this country that many men don't go to church; they allow their wives and children to go to church. While the women go to church, the men either stay at home or go fishing or doing something else. Many of these men have been deceived in their minds, thinking as long as my wife is praying for me, I am okay. They are not okay, because salvation and faith are personal

You have to first of all, become a believer and start to work out your salvation and faith as a child of God. As a Christian you have to own that faith, and be intentional in exercising it. You also have to know how to use and grow that faith. In fact, you have to make sure your faith is not missing in action. Sometimes as Christians we misplace our faith. You don't really lose it, but when you're not using your faith, it is missing in action. Jesus Christ once said to His disciples *"Where is your faith?"* (Lk 18:25)

Where did you put it? Let's establish this principle further. When you look at the gospel, there are many scriptures relating to the subject of faith. Sometimes the Lord Jesus Christ would say:

"Daughter, thy faith has made you whole" (Mark 5:34).

Many of us know about that, but I want to talk about three pronouns, and these are: *Our faith, Your faith, and Thy faith*. When you look at Luke 17: 5 The Lord Jesus was talking about forgiveness from verses 1-4, and in verse 5 there was a sudden interjection:

"And the apostles said unto the Lord, Increase our faith."

Now some of you may not know this, you need faith to forgive. You require faith because often times you're not going to feel you have forgiven. You have to believe, choose to forgive, and forgive by faith. In Hebrews 10:23 we are told:

"Let us hold fast the profession of our faith without wavering; (for he is faithful that promised ;)"

You are to hold on to the confession of your faith without wavering, and you must do this by:

"Looking unto Jesus the author and finisher of our faith;" (Hebrews 12:2)

We also see in 1 John 5:4 that:

"...whatsoever is born of God overcometh the world, and this is the victory that overcometh the world, even our faith".

So what is this our faith? Our faith is a combination of what I said the first time. The faith, which is our most holy faith, must attract our attention. So it's a collective noun, pronoun "our" faith. This means as a Christian, there should be no difference between your faith and my faith, it is the same thing. The 'DNA' of your faith is the same 'DNA' of my faith. The root of your faith is the root of my faith. So our faith is the same. That is why we say, sister or brother, let us agree together in prayer.

"Again I say unto you, That if two of you shall agree on earth as touching anything that they shall ask, it shall be done for them of my Father which is in heaven." (Matthew 18:19).

If two of you shall come together and agree, the Lord said I will do it for you because of your faith. So our faith is a potent faith. Any faith outside of Jesus is no faith. True faith is rooted in the Lord Jesus Christ. There is no one comparable to Jesus; even the devil knows it that there is no one like Jesus. So as a Christian, don't give up when you are down. No matter how you feel no matter what you're going through, don't give up because your faith is a great faith, it is an unbeatable faith, it cannot be defeated, and our faith is the victory that overcomes the world.

Do you know that if you don't believe in God, God believes in Himself? The unbelief of men cannot change the faith of God. If you don't believe in God, God cannot deny himself (2 Timothy 2:13). That is why you cannot stop God and His, work, because He has a plan, and his plan will be executed.

Our faith, that collective faith is the collation of our individual personal faith. That is your faith, my faith, and the congregational or corporate faith of the whole church when we come together is an overcoming faith, and that is very important to understand.

Whatsoever is born of God, what does that mean? It means if you are born of God, if you are born again, or if you are a new creation, old things are passed away, and all things have become new (2 Corinthians 5:17). If you have become a new person, that person who is born of God overcomes the world. How? The victory that overcomes the world is by our faith. You must exercise your faith to overcome because you have to resist the devil after submitting to God as we read in James 4:7:

"Submit yourselves therefore to God. Resist the devil, and he will flee from you."

You may be in the exam hall, and the devil is attacking your mind to a standstill but at that time you can't pick up your phone to call your pastor. You have to resist him saying "In Jesus name I will pass this course, and say amen to yourself."

For example, in my senior year in college, I was defending my thesis, when suddenly my supervisor began to mark me down. He started from A, he said I have five points against you, 5 points, negative in this project. But I was an A student who was supposed to get an "A". Further-more he talked about point 1, point 2, when he got to point 3, I said to myself "Devil you are a liar". This man was about to give me a "C". Under my breath, I commanded in the name of the Lord Jesus and said "Stop now". The man didn't hear my prayer but God heard, and so he did not go beyond the third point, he stopped. Thank God I had my faith available to exercise, because at that point in time my pastor was not nearby to help me. I ended up getting a "B". But if I had not prayed, he would have given me a "C".

To receive what I got I had to fight, and that is what life is about and why we need to put our faith to work. I had to use my faith, because I wasn't there to watch him mark me down, so I fought the devil with my faith. He may never know what happened to him, but I knew what I did with the power of God in my mouth, and the faith of God within me!

In case you don't know before now, your faith is an overcoming faith. You can overcome the devil, sickness, depression or anything that confronts you. The bible tells us in Galatians 2:20-21:

"I am crucified with Christ: nevertheless, I live; yet not I, but Christ liveth in me: and the life which I now live in the flesh I live by the faith of the Son of God, who loved me, and gave himself for me. I do not frustrate the grace of God: for if righteousness come by the law, then Christ is dead in vain."

There's a powerful truth here stated in verse 20 that many of us need to understand. The faith you exercise as a Christian is not your faith, it is the faith of Jesus. If you have received Jesus into your heart, you have faith now that is greater than you, sickness, poverty and bondage. When you are born again, you receive the spirit of God. It is that spirit that the bible is talking about here. *The power of the Holy Spirit is the power of faith.* So the life you live is not by your intellect, or the way you reason, by what you see, by what you hear or by what you feel. That is why the just, who has been changed by the power of the Holy Spirit, shall live by the faith of the Son of God, or specifically the faith of Jesus (Gal 2:20). Thus the Lord Jesus said:

"And these signs shall follow them that believe; In my name shall they cast out devils; they shall speak with new tongues;

They shall take up serpents; and if they drink any deadly thing, it shall not hurt them; they shall lay hands on the sick, and they shall recover." (Mark 16:17-18)

If you believe, everything Jesus did, you can do. In fact, you should be doing it. Everything you see in the gospels that the Lord Jesus did, every believer should be doing it. Why? Because the life we live is by the faith of the Lord Jesus Christ. To the point in which you can look at the storms of life and not fear, but like the eagle, you face the storm with boldness and say "*I shall not die but live and declare the works of the Lord" in the land of the living*" (Psalm 118:17).

Earlier this year, I preached on hope, and I said, "Don't give up, don't give in, don't go out, and don't go down." Even when you do go down, don't go out. You know in boxing, we have technical knockout, TKO. Sometimes the devil will give you as a believer, a TKO, don't be counted out. Before the count reaches ten get up, and don't be counted out. Micah in Chapter 7:8 says:

"***Rejoice not against me, O mine enemy: when I fall, I shall arise;***"

And Proverbs 24:16 affirms that "*... a just man falleth seven times, and riseth up again: but the wicked shall fall into mischief.*" In Job 14:7, we are told that there is hope for a tree even if the devil cuts it down, all it needs is the scent of water and it'll sprout again.

The faith you have is the faith of Jesus. It is an overcoming faith, it is a successful faith and it is a personal faith. This is the reason why you must own it, and not play with Jesus' command. There should be no time for frivolities or games. You have to take it seriously and own it as you build up yourself on your most holy faith (Jude 20). When you look at the gospel, you see the Lord Jesus saying: "***Be it unto you according to your faith.***" (Matthew 9:29).

Suffice it to say that God really responds to and takes our faith in Him seriously. This is akin to the passage in Numbers 14:28:

"Say unto them, As truly as I live, saith the Lord, as ye have spoken in mine ears, so will I do to you…".

Clearly we speak what we believe. When the blind men said "Yea Lord" as a mark of their faith that the Lord Jesus is able to heal them, he said *"According to your faith be it unto you"*.

Your faith has made you whole. But in Luke 8:25 mentioned earlier, we read:

"And he said unto them, Where is your faith? And they being afraid wondered saying one to another, What manner of man is this! that he commanded even the winds and water, and they obey him."

The story was that the disciples and the Lord Jesus were travelling on the same boat. A storm of wind arose while the Lord Jesus was sleeping in the boat, and it carried water into the boat. The disciples were so afraid that they ran to wake Him up from sleep saying:

"…Master, master, we perish. Then he arose, and rebuked the wind and the raging of the water: and they ceased, and there was a calm." (Lk 8:24)

We see the Master in this passage demonstrating His power over the elements - He rebuked the wind and the raging of the water, and there was a great calm. Then He turned unto them and said, where is your faith? The issue here is this, that the biggest battle a Christian fights is the battle of faith. And this is what happens; faith has an enemy instigated by the devil. That enemy is called "fear". F E A R aka False Evidence Appearing Real. I had a firsthand experience of the spirit of fear many years ago, and it took the intervention of God to deliver me.

In 1994 I lived in London, England, I came to the U.S., and I did a lot of traveling. All together I did about sixteen trips. One morning I came from Nashville to Pittsburgh, PA but I was actually going to West Virginia. I flew in that afternoon and my plane took off about 3 and about 3:20 there was a plane crash at Pittsburgh. I got to West Virginia, visited with the research group I came to meet and having done everything I had to do, I got to my motel room at about 6pm, turned on the TV then I heard on the news that there had been a plane crash at the airport that I left that afternoon.

I had an experience that I have only had once in my life and I will not have it again in Jesus name. As I was there in that room listening to the news, half way during the news, an atmosphere came over me. I turned off the T.V. I said "God what am I going to do?" I am supposed to go back to London tomorrow, how am I going to fly in this funny propeller plane? Fear came all over me, and I am telling you a true story. If it were possible to drive, from Morgantown, West Virginia back to London I would have done it. Fear came upon me, I have never experienced that kind of thing before, I was so scared, and I could not even listen to the news anymore. I began to say "Okay God, how do I get home? How do I go back to London? But I can't drive from Morgantown to Pittsburgh and catch a flight from Pittsburgh to London. How will I do that? So I was just there, paralyzed with fear.

Then all of a sudden, oh thank God for the Holy Ghost something quickened inside my spirit and said you're a Christian, you're a believer, you are afraid. I said "Devil you are a liar, *I rebuke you spirit of fear*" *and it lifted.* So I learned a profound truth that day. Fear is a spirit. Fear is not a feeling, and it is from the devil. Fear is the opposite and the enemy of faith. This is the point I am trying to make. If you entertain or give room to fear, you cannot have faith. It is fear that causes you to have panic attack, anxiety and sleepless nights. That is fear, it is not faith.

Fear drives your faith away, so don't give room to fear. No matter what you are going through, fear not, because your faith is an overcoming faith. You will overcome in Jesus name. Don't give in to fear of who you'll marry, fear of a Job, fear of what you'll eat, but rebuke fear in the name of the Lord Jesus Christ. Banish fear from your life. However, the truth is that statistically, 85% of what we fear never happen. "O God am I going to live alone the rest of my life?" You will not be alone. God will give you a wife; God will give you a husband. What will happen to my children if they go to college? Fear not, Angels will watch over your children when you are not there. God is able to keep them.

All the things you are afraid of will never happen in Jesus name. So don't give room to fear. The bible says in Romans 4:20 Abraham staggered not in faith because he didn't give in to fear. It was Sarah who encouraged Abraham to go to Haggai because she felt that God was delaying; they both made a terrible mistake in doing so, and thereby brought forth Ishmael. It's still a problem till today. Don't create a problem out of fear. Don't go and marry the wrong man or woman out of fear. Don't go and take a job or go into business out of fear. Don't do anything out of fear. Don't give room to fear "*...all things are possible to him that believes*" (Mark 9:23).

Allow your personal faith to speak. This is a dimension of the Christian faith that many of us don't really know how powerful it is. Your personal faith can affect a whole family, and can change culture. When you look at the scriptures especially the epistles of Paul to the Romans, 1 Corinthians, 2 Corinthians, 1 Thessalonians, and Colossians you will hear this phrase "*...your faith is proclaimed*" or "*we have heard of your faith*", or "*your faith is spread abroad*". In the letter to the Ephesians and Colossians, Paul shows that the proclamation of their faith provoked thanksgiving and prayers constantly for them (Ephesians 1:15-18, Colossians 1:4).

Rejoicing over the steadfastness of their faith, he again exhorted them to become rooted and built up in the Lord Jesus Christ and established in their faith (Colossians 2:5-7). Unknown to you, by standing firm as a Christian there are people who would be encouraged by your action.

One of the things that shocked me when I signed on Facebook was the fact that within a year or two I started connecting with some of my old high school classmates that I had not seen or heard from since 1978. What also shocked me was the fact that these guys had been thinking about me all these years. One of them said "Nosa, last Sunday I was just using you to preach here in my church".

It triggered a remembrance of another incident that occurred at the end of my freshman year in college, the Christians in my class often met to pray in the evenings. One evening, one of us who was a younger Christian read how the Lord Jesus turned water to wine. He then said he is believing that God can use us to do the same. Those of us who were more matured as Christians in order not to discourage his faith although taken aback, just played along. We really believed, we said anything could happen. But I am going somewhere with this story.

We prayed and prayed for hours, but the water did not turn to wine, okay? But this is what happened, when the older Christians on the other side of the campus heard, they were provoked. It provoked something in their spirit, that if a young Christian can choose to believe in God to turn water to wine, then what are we doing? Then their faith began to grow. What I am trying to pass across to you is that, your faith has impact. Whether you believe it or not, the way you live now affects those around you, because they are watching you. I never preached to most of my siblings, they just observed me, but today they are all Christians.

No matter your story, brethren even if the devil gives you a TKO, don't stay down, get up and fight. This is because there are people that the bible says are waiting to see your manifestation in Romans 8:19:

"For the earnest expectation of the creature waiteth for the manifestation of the sons of God."

And they're in pains and they're groaning as v22 tells us. There are people who are waiting for you to manifest. You must manifest in Jesus name.

Your faith is impactful. Your faith is a powerful faith. You have no clue the tens of thousands, hundreds of thousands, maybe even millions waiting for you to manifest. Don't give up but have a propelling power and force to overcome the world. Paul writing to the Corinthians (1 Corinthians 2:4-5) stressed that his preaching was not with enticing words of man's wisdom, but in demonstration of the Spirit and of power, "*That your faith should not stand in the wisdom of men, but in the power of God*".

Faith that would stand the test of time must be based on the power of God. This power of God demonstrated by the resurrection of the Lord Jesus now provides the foundation for their faith not being in vain. Thus the veracity of their faith is based on the resurrection of the Lord Jesus Christ. Otherwise if there is no resurrection, then their faith would be in vain. The Lord Jesus Christ is risen and alive today, and declared to be the Son of God by the His resurrection from the dead (Romans 1:4). Whilst correcting the Corinthians (2 Corinthians 1:23-24), Paul comments that their role as spiritual leaders was not to be domineering or dictators over "*your faith*", but helpers of "*...your joy...*".

He clearly shows us here the importance of the need for Spiritual leaders to avoid dictatorial tendencies in leadership. "*...For by faith ye stand*". Paul's hope for them as they stand in faith was "*...when your faith is increased...*", the boundaries of their ministry will be extended and enlarged – 2 Corinthians 10:15. In his first epistle to the Thessalonians (1 Thessalonians 1:8 and 3:2-10), we observe these principles:

- "*...your faith is spread abroad...*" just like in the case of the Romans, Ephesians and Colossians.
- As a result Paul sent Timothy with the singular purpose to:
  o "*...establish you and to comfort you concerning your faith...*"
  o "*...sent to know your faith...*" to know how their faith was bearing under intense pressure.
- When Timothy came back, he brought "*...good tidings of your (steadfast) faith...*"

- These good tidings brought comfort "*...in our affliction and distress by your faith*"
- The effect of the comforting news provoked earnest praying night and day to see their face and "*...might perfect that which is lacking in your faith*".

In 2 Thessalonians 1:3-4, Paul had gone beyond perfecting their faith to thanking God and glorying in the fact that "*...your faith groweth exceedingly...*"

So we see in scriptures that faith is personal. This faith can grow because there is a seed in it. This faith will face trials. James 1:3 says "*...the trying of your faith works patience*". What is the lesson? This faith that is your personal faith will be tried. For your faith to grow, it must be tested. You must face a challenge; the challenge is to take you to a higher ground. Please don't forget this truth because as believers when we face challenges in life we start giving up on God. No, don't give up; the purpose of the trial of your faith is to develop you in patience and patience having her perfect work, to produce maturity in you.

"But let patience have her perfect work that you may be perfect and entire wanting nothing." (James 1:4)

So your personal faith will be tried to grow your faith. You have to be resolute in your faith. How can your faith grow? It is by exercising it. It is not every time you have a headache, you must go for Tylenol, or Advil. Not every time.

Next time you have it, say "I rebuke you in the name of Jesus, headache go." Forget it; you'll be surprised that you will even forget you had a headache. There's nothing wrong in taking medicine, but it's not every time you have headache that you pop pills. It's not every time you need money, that you say to yourself, I know if I call Sister J, she is going to give me money. Instead of this, pray and say "Lord provide for me." Let

God send a stranger to bless me. One day, expect the IRS to pay you all that they owe you and know how God can provide.

I have experienced that before many years ago. No job, no business, suddenly in the mail was an IRS check for about $4,500 owed to me. When they owe you, they pay you with interest. They owed me over $3,000 and they paid me about $1,500 interest. So you have to believe your faith is going to produce for you, for the trial of your faith works patience, praise the name of the Lord. Peter says it,

"That the trial of your faith, being much more precious than of gold that perisheth..." (1 Peter 1:7)

Peter in his second epistle (2 Peter 1:5) encourages us to make every effort in exercising *"your faith"*, to develop (add) virtue (moral excellence) to your faith. When we look at the gospels, we see the woman with the issue of blood, Jesus said to her, *"...Thy faith has made you whole"* (Matthew 9:22, Mark 5:34, Luke 8:48).

We also see the blind men, the Lord Jesus asked them, *"Do you believe?"* They said, *"Yes Lord we do believe"* (Matthew 9:28) Be it unto you according to your faith. God responds primarily to faith. You want to get things from God, it is by faith. The way to change your life is by your faith. The way to progress and move forward in life is by your faith, because the just shall live by faith. So we see it is your personal faith. In the case of blind Bartimaeus (Mark 10:52, Luke 18:42), the Lord Jesus said unto him "...*Thy faith has made thee whole...*" in the Mark passage and "...*Thy faith hath saved thee...*" in the Luke passage. Salvation (Soteria in Greek) means wholeness/ Completeness (Shalom – nothing missing and nothing broken) in your Spirit, Soul and Body.

There is nothing wrong in asking men to pray for you, I believe in that. I ask people to pray for me, but often times, God will be saying. "Pray for yourself." Learn how to pray for yourself and get answers to your prayer, because faith is personal. So know how to conquer fear by faith.

When you don't use your faith, your faith will not grow. Learn to ask God for what your faith is able to believe for now, before believing for something bigger.

Let me tell you as a young Christian, I was a teenager and often times I would have ten or twenty cents in my pocket and would need a taxi to go to church. So this is what I used to do. "Taxi, taxi, taxi! I am going to XYZ how much is my fare?" He would answer "Twenty cents for the trip", and I would reply "Ten cents? Since I only had ten cents with me." On hearing my response, they would just drive away. Then I would just pray, "Lord give me a taxi driver that will agree to take Ten cents." A taxi would come, and I would say "How much?" "He would say Twenty cents", I would reply "Ten cents, as I only had Ten cents." He would surprisingly respond "Enter!" Many times I went to church with Ten cents in my pocket and God answered my prayers.

Now we can believe God for more and for a debt free life both in our personal lives as well as in ministry. We need finances for the work of the ministry both at home and on the mission field. Pastor Anne and I were in London one day at Kingsway International Christian Centre (KICC), and people were coming out to give towards the building funds - 100 pounds, 200 pounds, and 500 pounds etc. I didn't know if we could afford up to 50 pounds, you know what she did? She left the church, went outside, and cried to God, and said "If you bless me, I will use my money to build your house." So when people do things, you don't know where they are coming from. You don't know the prayer they have prayed. That's why she will be blessed. Because she went out and prayed a prayer that only God and herself and I know and said "God Bless Me" because she was weeping that she could not give for the work of God.

This is faith; you have to believe God to change your situation. Don't accept mediocrity and say it doesn't matter, that's where we are. It matters and that's not where you are. God wants to move you further in Jesus name, Amen. Your faith saves you, you live by faith, you overcome by faith, and your faith must not fail. When you read the story of the woman with the alabaster box in Luke 7:44-48 Jesus said:

"And he turned to the woman, and said unto Simon, Seest thou this woman? I entered into thine house, thou gavest me no water for my feet: but she hath washed my feet with tears, and wiped them with the hairs of her head.

Thou gavest me no kiss: but this woman since the time I came in hath not ceased to kiss my feet.

My head with oil thou didst not anoint: but this woman hath anointed my feet with ointment.

Wherefore I say unto thee, Her sins, which are many, are forgiven; for she loved much: but to whom little is forgiven, the same loveth little.

And he said unto her, Thy sins are forgiven."

What was the secret of that woman who was a community sinner? The bible says when she knew that Jesus was in the house, she came with her alabaster box. What was the key there? She believed in Jesus enough to use a whole year's wages to buy perfumed olive oil to anoint Him. This is because she did not use the normal or regular olive oil; she bought the most expensive oil. That was why Jesus said Simon, even the regular olive oil, you didn't anoint me with, but this woman spent one year's wages to buy oil to anoint me. It wasn't about the ointment but it was more about her faith in Jesus.

And that's why Jesus said in Luke 7:50, "...*thy faith hath saved thee...*". He didn't say your alabaster box saved you. It was because she believed she was able to give. Why is it that when we talk about everything Christians shout, but when we talk about money, we go silent? It is unbelief. If a Christian feels uncomfortable about money, it is unbelief.

If you believe in Jesus, let me tell you, you can't wait to give to the work of the ministry as God has blessed you.

We see from the foregoing that you can be healed, saved and made whole by "**Thy Faith**". Finally, Jude 20 says:

"Build up yourself on your most Holy faith, praying in the Holy Ghost."

Put your hands on your belly and begin to pray in the Holy Ghost that your faith will be strong and grow.

CHAPTER 5

The Prepositions of Faith – Faith Is Tangible

As we proceed on our journey of understanding faith and its attributes, let us begin by stating the fact that faith is tangible. It is a material, real; it is neither guess work, nor philosophy. It is very important for you to understand that for a Christian, faith is a tangible thing. Therefore, if faith is a material, and tangible, what am I supposed to do? You develop and use it. In the last chapter, we learnt about the challenge the Lord Jesus posed to the disciples asking them *"where is your faith?"* This in essence meant that the disciples had either hidden their faith, or not used it.

You cannot afford to put your faith on the shelf, it must be put to work, that you may profit with it. You have a personal faith in Christ, and that personal faith is a force that is empowered to do exploits in Christ. *Therefore, faith is a tangible material that I must use to acquire my desire.* In Hebrews 11 we see two common refrains *"through faith"* we understand (vs. 3), and *"by faith"* Abel, Enoch, Noah, Abraham (vs. 4, 5, 7, 8) and so on and so forth. And after each name mentioned, what their faith made to happen was listed. These two words are the prepositions, *"by"* and *"through"*. But in biblical context, they have meaning. The first one we are examining is in verse 11 *"through faith also Sara"*. What does it mean? It means <u>because of faith</u> something happened to Sarah, which means if you have some elements of faith in your heart, God will do something for you.

It doesn't have to be big faith, but just because you have faith in your heart, you can have your desire. Sometimes, like Sarah we are human. God told her, you are going to have a son, and Sarah laughed, because she thought it was a joke, at age 90? She did not believe, but because the faith of Abraham was in the atmosphere, it happened as God said. Often times, we think we cannot receive because our faith is not big; it's not about size. That is why our Lord Jesus Christ said in Matthew 17:20 that:

"... If ye have faith as a grain of mustard seed, ye shall say unto this mountain, remove hence to yonder place; and it shall remove; and nothing shall be impossible unto you."

The reason God will do it is *because you believe*, not because your faith was big. A great man of God who is gone to Heaven now, who grew up in my city, told this story to some of his ministers and I got to hear it. He had a stadium crusade in East Africa, many years ago. The stadium was packed full. He said as a human being, if the cripples, blind, and deaf, they brought were in the crowd, it would have been easier to preach God can heal you. But they brought them to the platform, so you can't run away. Man of God, if you say God will heal, we want to see it today.

So they brought cripples, blind, lame, not in the crowd, but they lined them up on the platform. He said honestly at that moment, he didn't think he had enough faith to believe God. This was a great man of God sharing his experience, but according to him, he kept on preaching until he could no longer extend the sermon. There had to be a performance, and the people were waiting and watching his next move. As a human being in that moment, he really didn't have enough faith to heal all of those people, so he said to the crowd, "Do you believe God can heal?" The whole stadium roared and said yes! He said start to pray, and he was still marking time. This was the late Archbishop Benson Idahosa.

So they began to pray and he too was praying. He didn't know what to do. O blessed be the name of the Lord, as the congregation began to pray, the power of God came upon him, and he didn't have to touch them as he began to speak the word of faith - "Cripple, I command you to get up and walk." and the cripples began to jump up and walk. God saw his faith and the faith of the people and he did something, when it looked impossible humanly speaking.

God will step into your situation. So when we look at Hebrews 11, what does "*by faith*" mean? It means, *through the agency of faith, using faith as an instrument, and faith as a means to do something.* So for instance you want your Daddy to buy something for you, you clean the house and say Daddy, I have cleaned the house, give me some money, isn't it? You believe that when you clean the house, your Daddy will give you some money, that's faith. It's a means to something; faith is an instrument you have as a believer to make things happen for you. That is why the just shall live by faith, because every aspect of your life has to be orchestrated by your faith in God.

Whether it is for your exams, healing, bearing children, prosperity, and protection, you must have faith in God. Everything in the kingdom hinges on faith, and faith is the currency of the kingdom of God. It is the means of transaction, for without faith, you cannot transact business in the kingdom of God. In fact, without faith you wouldn't even be a Christian, for we are saved by grace through (the agency of) faith. That is what Ephesians 2:8-9 tell us. We are saved by grace *through faith.* Through the agency of faith, the carrier and the instrument that help us to execute what we believe. This is powerful; faith can cause things to happen for you in Jesus name.

Through that simple word "by", God will cause things to happen. That is what the bible means when it says by faith. What happened there for all of those heroes of faith from Abraham, to Jacob, Noah, Isaac, Elijah, Elisha, David, and to Daniel, all they did was by faith. By their faith they caused things to happen. Why would Shadrach, Meshach and Abednego step into the fire, if they were not willing to die? Obviously they were not afraid to die, but when they stepped into the fire, their faith caused the fire to become air condition. When you have faith in God, it will change your situation. God can turn your life around 180 degrees. By faith, God can cause your enemies to be at peace with you, your boss to give you double promotion and you recover all you have lost in ten years. Faith is a force. There are two powerful behavioral forces:

1. **Love** - the most important and many of us don't even know this. Love is a spiritual force. When you love people and they hate you, don't worry, you will always win. When you love people and they do you wrong, don't worry, because love is more powerful than hate. Keep loving them, a day will come; the person will not be able to resist your love anymore.

2. *Faith* - is a force. Faith is a spiritual force. When you exercise faith, the devil will run. When you have faith, you will always win, when you have faith you will not quit, and because you don't quit, you will win. For through patience and endurance, you will obtain the promise. So <u>through</u>, faith, things happen, and <u>by the agency of</u> faith God will heal you. As a Christian, you must change your tactics, speak faith, and speak life into what you want in your situation. There are such things called the words of faith, unbelief, fear, anger, and ignorance. When you release the word of faith, angels begin to work on your behalf. Paul said, "**We believe, therefore we speak.**" (2 Corinthians 4:13).

If you believe, God will heal you, then speak it out saying "I am healed in Jesus name." if you believe God will prosper you, say it loud in Jesus name. If you believe, say it, because through that faith, God will make things to happen.

There are many scriptures we can look at, but let's just start with Acts 15:9-26. We see here that by faith, our hearts are purified, and by faith we are sanctified. When you get saved, you didn't see an angel using a sponge to wash your heart. How did you know your heart is clean? By faith you believe, and how did you know your sins are forgiven? How did you know you stand righteous in God? by faith. So Romans

3:22, 28, 30 declares that we have our righteousness, by faith, and a lot of scriptures speak to the fact that we are justified. Just as if we never committed any sin. In Romans 5:1, we read:

"Therefore being justified by faith, we have peace with God..."

All these scriptures focus on the word "by", as we see in verse 2:

"By whom also we have access by faith into this grace wherein we stand..." vs. 2.

When you are born again as a child of God, this is what happens verse 2 says by Him, by the Lord Jesus Christ, we have access by faith, into this grace, wherein we stand and rejoice in hope of the glory of God. The day the Lord Jesus said on the cross, *"It is finished"* many things happened, and one of the most significant things, as a Christian you need to understand, that happened was that the veil of the temple was torn from the top to bottom into two:

"Jesus, when he had cried again with a loud voice, yielded up the ghost.

And, behold, the veil of the temple was rent in twain from the top to the bottom; and the earth did quake, and the rocks rent;" (Matt 27:50-51).

What does that mean? Until Jesus died, only the high priests could go beyond the veil. The bible says *"...the veil of the temple was rent in twain.."* But this is the powerful thing, it was not any man/woman who rent the curtain in two, nor was it split from the bottom to the top.

"For by grace are ye saved through faith; and that not of yourselves: it is the gift of God:

Not of works, lest any man should boast" (Ephesians 2:8-9)

You couldn't work for it. God did it all and that is why He rent the temple veil from the **top** to the **bottom**. You couldn't have boasted about your salvation, God did it Himself. I say now you have access. This signature alone is enough to get you on fire for God. Go home, talk to God, He will hear your prayers.

I know what it means to believe God, all alone by yourself when no one believed in you. By this faith I have access to God. I can talk to him anywhere that I am because I have access to the Kingdom of God. Therefore, I can sing:

Father we have confidence by the blood of Jesus. To come into the place where you are (2ce)

One of the pictures I brag about concerning my generation is shown below. A group of us in high school, some in 6th, 7th, and 8th grades but I was in 9th grade. There were also a couple of 10th, 11th and 12th graders included in that photograph. Let me briefly share with you the story behind that picture. We were all about 150 - 200 high school kids that belonged to a Christian Fellowship group. To a lot of people, we were a bunch of crazy kids. They used to taunt us saying "Look at them S. U. people (aka -Scripture Union)." In spite of all these pressure groups resisting our existence, what surprised me the most was that none of us was intimidated in any way or form because the power is in the seed. In that photograph there are 6th graders and 7th graders who today are pastors.

What do you think a 6th grader knows about Jesus? All they had was a little faith. They didn't know where God was going to take them. In that photograph, probably somewhere about 10 to 20 of us didn't know what God had in His mind for us. We looked foolish but we just had simple faith. We went to church, we read the bible, we sang hallelujah and we went home. To some people it was a joke, but blessed be the name of the Lord now the reality is here! When I look at that photograph of us in high school, who would have known that some of us would become pastors and teachers or something significant?

For by faith you have access into something that is spiritual and heavenly. The Kingdom of God is a superior Kingdom. For by faith we stand. Why do we fall as Christians? We fall when our faith is weak! We stand by faith, you see that in 2 Cor. 1:24, and 1 Cor. 2:5. We stand in the power of God. The power of God is the foundation and assurance of our faith. We walk by faith - 2 Cor 5:7. With our faith, we can stand strong as Christians. Storms will come, winds will blow, the rain will fall and unless you are standing tall on the rock, unless you are constantly obeying and doing His will, so that you build your life on Jesus, you cannot stand.

I am standing today because of the word of God. Without the word of God, I would have been history a long time ago. I have fought battles since I was young, as a teenager, as a young adult and as a married man. As a father, as a husband, as a pastor, I've fought so many battles. Fighting the battles of life is why we will win in Jesus name. For by faith we stand. If you fall, get up back again and stand. Stand by faith. Christ dwells in our hearts by faith." Sometimes the devil will tell you, you are no longer a Christian, but don't believe anything he says. You are still a child of God, for Jesus dwells in your heart by faith - Ephesians 3:17. Furthermore, 2 Corinthians 5:7 says - "*For we walk by faith and not by sight.*"

This means; you regulate your life by faith. You conduct your life by faith, by a conviction. You do not run your life just by what you see, feel or hear, but by what God has said in His word concerning any particular circumstance. The God we serve is unchangeable, He is consistent. In Acts 3:16 we read the fact that by faith, miracles happen, and by faith Jesus is our substitute lamb through which we are saved. By faith we have revelation of God and His promises for us. You need faith to know God. The reason many of us don't grow in God is because we don't grow in our faith, we don't exercise our faith. There are certain things you will not know about God until you exercise your faith. You need faith to understand. That's why people argue, was the world created? Was there evolution? I believe that God created the heavens and the earth.

Do you really believe you came from an ape or from an amoeba? When I was in school they told us the smallest living thing was a cell. Current science has proven that a cell is a system. Scientists got confused, they said that the Big Bang Theory cannot be this structured or organized. As a designer, I have a doctrine in design. I understand that there is such a thing as design intent. There is a reason chlorophyll is green. There is a reason for everything in creation. There is a reason the fish can swim at speeds we cannot comprehend, a reason an eagle can spread its wings and soar. It's because every work of creation has design intent.

So by faith we understand that God created all living creatures. What is the summary? Your faith is tangible. Don't let the devil deceive you, you have faith, and your faith can give you strength. Before you start getting worried about the future say, Lord I trust you, I commit my future in your hands. As a young man I worried a lot about my future and whenever that happened I would sing this song to myself.

Song:

>   Many things about tomorrow
>   I don't seem to understand
>   But I know who holds tomorrow
>   And I know who holds my hands

At other times when I was worried I sang this song

Song:
> Because He lives, I can face tomorrow
> Because He lives, All fear is gone.
> Because I know He holds the future
> And life is worth the living just because He lives.

No matter what happens to you in life don't give up on life. Say because He lives I can face tomorrow. God sometimes will not do things the way you want them, it is okay you don't have to be in control. Just because God did not answer your prayer the way you want it does not mean God will not answer it His own way. A Christian must and should walk in faith! Don't walk by what you see, just believe that God has a greater purpose for you! It is well.

In the exegesis of the prepositions of "by faith" and "through faith", Romans 3:30 gives us a foundational basis. Paul points out here the intersection of justification of both Jews (circumcised) and Gentiles (uncircumcised) by faith and through faith respectively. **The Jews** being justified "**by faith**" which originated and began with Abraham and **the Gentiles** being justified "**through** (the channel and because of their newly acquired) faith".

CHAPTER 6

The Heroes of Faith

As we begin to examine the heroes of faith in this chapter, our focus text is Hebrews 11. There are certain scriptures that can preach on their own. This is one of those scriptures; all you need is just to read it. It is a message in itself, and there are lots of riches and wealth in these scriptures. Hebrews 11 is the book or chapter of faith and what you see in this chapter are examples of real people who worked out their faith in the bible. These are not fairy tales, but people just like you and I. Their stories are catalogued in this hall of fame of Faith. There are some people who dream of being in the NBA, NFL or other sporting halls of fame. Others are in the music hall of fame, or acclaimed in many other endeavors.

No matter the hall of fame you belong, the one in Hebrews 11 is the most important hall of fame anyone would want to belong to. This one was compiled by God, it solely depends on Him, and you don't need a special qualification to be on that list. You can be a man or a woman, a boy, or a girl, you can be young or old, and all you need is faith in God to belong to this category.

This hall of fame cannot be said to have been completed without you and I added to the list. That is prophetically, this chapter of the bible is not complete without you. This means you are supposed to write your own story of exploits of faith in this chapter. Briefly have an introspection of the story of your life, where you were, where you are now and where you need to be. This is the chapter that defines faith. In Hebrews 11:1-2 we read:

"Now faith is the substance of things hoped for, the evidence of things not seen. For by it the elders obtained a good report."

The verse 2 of it again confirms the position that faith is personal. With your faith you are supposed to produce a good report in the history of mankind. For example, Shakespeare said, "The world is a stage, and we are all actors in it." From Africa to Europe, from Australia to Antarctica, from the North Pole to the South Pole, from Johannesburg to London, from Sydney to Beijing China, the world is a stage and we are all actors in it. This is a true statement. The world is a stage where we are all acting, and creating history. Don't forget this very important point.

In fact, this generation cannot ever escape it, because everyone has some form of record on the internet, one way or the other. In this generation, even if you didn't know it, you are making history. One hundred years from now people are perhaps going to read about you. The question is when they open your book, what are they going to read about you? Is it something encouraging or disturbing?

Please know for a fact that it's not truly about how long you lived, it's about how well you have lived. One of my favorite pastors has gone to heaven a long time ago. He is Robert Murray M' Cheyne (1813 – 1843), who oversaw a congregation in Dundee, Scotland.

This man started to pastor at twenty-two years old. He was a pastor over the congregation for seven years, and died at the age of 29. Up to this day, many seminaries are still learning about his sermons. His sermons outlived him, and became legacy sermons. So are you writing or making history? Are you building legacies or monuments? Legacies last, but monuments collapse after sometime, never to be remembered again. If you are building legacies, then you belong to this hall of fame.

However, know that every challenge you are facing in life is part of your making history. All the problems you have faced are to help you produce a good report. So stop complaining and don't envy anybody.

Proverbs 22:29 asks us a profound question and follows it up with a thoughtful revelation:

"Seest thou a man diligent in his business? he shall stand before kings; he shall not stand before mean men."

Diligence in business is anchored in and by faith. Because you believe in the outcome, you're willing to put in so much, with the expectation of the reward or fruits. When the bible talks about heroes of faith, what do you think was propelling them? They were urged on, they were prompted, they were stirred up by faith. Because they had faith in God, they did something. You cannot have faith, see the light and do nothing. *Faith is actionable*; faith will give you the strength to do something productive. The bible says in Hebrews 11:19 amplified version that Abraham:

"...considered [it reasonable to believe] that God was able to raise Isaac even from among the dead. [Indeed, in the sense that he was prepared to sacrifice Isaac in obedience to God] Abraham did receive him back [from the dead] figuratively speaking."

The point here is that Abraham had made up his mind to sacrifice Isaac because he knew that God would bring him back to life, he had faith. His sacrifice was obedience to God. *"For by faith, Isaac blessed Jacob and Esau"* (vs 20), and urged on by faith, Jacob blessed his sons, (vs 21) by faith Joseph, when he was about to die spoke of something that he had not seen. Joseph saw by faith, with the eye of faith, he knew that Egypt was not their destination and that God was going to take them out of Egypt. So he said when God takes you out, carry my bones, take them out of Egypt, and take them to the Promised Land. How did Joseph know that? This event described occurred about 400 plus years later. How did Joseph know? It was by faith. This teaches us that as Christians we should live by faith. That means you must take action based on faith.

You take action about your future based on faith, not based on feeling, or reaction to what you hear on the news. Have faith in God, before you react, think about God first. So make decisions about your future based on faith, not based on feelings, not based on just what you see.

"By faith Moses, when he was born, was hid three months of his parents, because they saw he was a proper child;......" (Hebrews 11:23)

When he was born his mother reasoned that other children were just kids but Moses was a proper child. She was willing to take a risk, and said to herself "I am going to put him in a basket, place him in River Nile and allow him to float." Meanwhile, his sister stood afar off to watch what would happen to him (Exodus 2:3-4). That was audacious faith at work. Believing that somehow there would be salvation for Moses, until miraculously the princess of Egypt came and found Moses. So by faith she hid him. From verse 24 we read:

"By faith Moses, when he was come to years, refused to be called the son of Pharaoh's daughter; Choosing rather to suffer affliction with the people of God, than to enjoy the pleasures of sin for a season;" (Hebrews 11:24-25).

What does verse 25 teach us? When a Christian is struggling with sin, it is an indication of unbelief. When you put one leg in the church and one leg in the kingdom of darkness, it is unbelief. You go to church today, and then tomorrow you go to either the psychic, or the native doctor. Or perhaps, you send a letter to India to ask for charms to be sent to you? If you are at that point in your life, and you are reading this book, please drop it now; kneel down before God in confession and repentance and request for deliverance. The fact of the matter here is that, if you cannot trust God to help you, and you're putting your faith in psychics, in necromancy, in native doctor, and in voodoo priest to help you then you need serious spiritual help.

Let it not be that you are named or numbered among such people. You are a pastor; you go and see a native doctor to give you special powers, what kind of pastor are you? You are depending on the arm of the flesh for help, and woe is upon those who do so. The moment you trust in yourself or in unbelievers, woe comes upon you. The moment you trust in man, woe comes upon you. There are three woes you must be afraid of in the bible. Woe to those that trust in Egypt, meaning trust in unbelievers (Isaiah 31:1). Woe to those that trust in the arm of the flesh, that means you trust in yourself, that means you have more faith in yourself and others than God (Jeremiah 17:5). You have brought judgment upon yourself, and the bible says "***Woe to him that puts his trust in man.***" (Jeremiah 17:5). That means you are more afraid of/or trust people than God. You need the help of God.

Learn to trust the Lord that He's faithful, and He is able to do what He promised. Can you imagine what Noah went through when he was told to build an ark? For one hundred years he never saw rain yet he kept building the ark. That is real faith at work. Don't you think many people will say this guy must either be foolish or mad? He is building an ark and there is no water for it to row on.

If you truly have faith in God, be consistent. How do I know you have faith? Your faithfulness in good times and in bad times is a great indicator. God remains committed to you no matter your situation. When you pass through the water or fire, God is there with you (Isaiah 43:2). He is consistent; your faith too must be consistent.

So we see here that Moses chose rather to suffer with Christians than to enjoy the sin of Egypt. That was faith in God. You see, many of us don't understand one major fact, that is what he gave up for standing with God! Do you know that Moses was raised in the most powerful house in the world at that time? He had everything at his beck and call, and yet he gave all that up because of his faith in God. That was some price paid there. He gave up the pleasure of the palace for the deprivation of ghetto life so-to-speak. He gave away his affluence, wealth, status and power because he believed in God. The true mark of a Christian is what will you exchange for your soul? There are some Christians that ended up in the trap unbelievers set for them because they were carried away by worldly riches. There are people today who say God; you can enter this house, this room, this living room, but my guest chamber and bar, no way! No, God it belongs to me, and I will do whatever I want with it. That's not faith. Faith is to trust God, no matter what. Will you do the right thing even if it will cost you your job? If your boss tells you to lie, will you say no, I am a Christian, I will not lie! Are you ready to lose your Job and say the truth as a Christian? That is faith.

As a sixteen and a half years old, the king in my city died and ALL the men in the whole city were mandated to shave their hair. It was mandatory culturally; every man had to shave because the king died. My paternal and maternal grandfathers, father, and uncle all shaved, but I stood my ground refusing to cut my hair for the dead. I am not telling you another person's story; I am telling you my own story.

There are things you need to do as a Christian to earn something in the kingdom. There are certain things when you do it, heaven recognizes you. At sixteen and a half years old, I defied my father, and that was the one time I disobeyed him. I defied my family. I refused to shave. For three weeks, I wore a shirt and a jeans pant, because I could not gain access to my suitcase in my father's house. He told me he could not have two masters in his house. "If you are not going to shave, leave my house." No problem, I would rather serve God than man, and I left his house that day. I went back to the campus and stayed with a brother.

The Christian faith is not a joke, we don't go to church to play, and church is not a game. There must be a time in your life when you would be required to take a stand, and when that time comes I pray you would not disappoint God. Continuing the story, my uncle who was a principal, was well respected and intimidating to the people in the whole city and you don't dare say "no" to him. He was shocked when I said no. Then he sat back, and he realized this boy must know something that I didn't know. I looked at his face in my grandfather's living room and said, "The bible says I shouldn't cut my hair for the dead, and I am not going to shave my head." He looked at me and just said "Okay".

God has to bring you to that point; just like Moses. Would you give up everything because of Jesus? The American Church doesn't know this today. We do what every person likes. Can you stand alone for Jesus? That is faith. When my high school friends heard about my story, it encouraged and challenged their faith. Why did I tell you my story? It is to hit home the impact of what Moses did. You read it but you may not think it was faith at work, but until you come to a point where your boss says change the figures on the books or you lose your job, what would you do? There are corrupt people everywhere, corrupt people in Africa, Europe, Asia, and America.

Last week, a man told us how he was shipping steel to the middle-east from America. They put half steel, half sand and shipped it until it got to the Middle East. So there are corrupt people everywhere, but will you do the right thing? So by faith Moses stood his ground. In verses 26 to 27 we read:

"Esteeming the reproach of Christ greater riches than the treasures in Egypt: for he had respect unto the recompence of the reward.

By faith he forsook Egypt, not fearing the wrath of the king: for he endured, as seeing him who is invisible."

By faith he forsook Egypt. Faith is the word of God, and with the word you can win anywhere. With the bible you can win in Russia, Johannesburg, Lagos, London and Dallas. The bible is all weather, in summer or winter, the bible is the same. Last year, the bible was the same. A thousand years ago, the bible was the same; a thousand years from now the bible will not change. Hold unto God, for God is not a man that he should lie, neither the son of a man that he should repent. I like this chapter because it is a balance of faith. In verses 29-30 we read

"By faith they passed through the Red sea as by dry land: which the Egyptians assaying to do were drowned.

By faith the walls of Jericho fell down, after they were compassed about seven days."

Going through the Red Sea is symbolic of your being washed in your sins. That is your sins are washed away and that's why when you go into the water as in baptism, you die, and your sins are buried. When you come out of the water, you are washed, you are a new man, a new creation, and you are justified just as if you never sinned. You are acquitted of guilt, with a clean slate, and if you die that way, you will go to heaven. You will go to heaven because of what Jesus did, not because of what you did. That is faith.

Secondly, you must enter your promised land. However, there are walls of Jericho that will want to prevent you from entering your promised land, so you have to have faith, to march around the walls of Jericho and speak to them until they collapse. Don't kick it, don't fight it, but you simply have to command it to fall down flat. Ask the ground by faith to open and swallow every opposition in your life in Jesus name. Every stronghold in your life, pull it down by faith in Jesus name. Resist everything and anything that resists your progress, promotion, and fruitfulness.

Anything that tries to hinder your progress is a wall of Jericho. So what must you do? You must believe God to pull it down. God will sink every opposition to your life in Jesus name. God will cause the ground to open and swallow any hindrance to your progress in Jesus name.

Now this is my favorite, in verse 31 we read:

"By faith the harlot Rahab perished not with them that believed not, when she had received the spies with peace." (Hebrews 11:31)

Prompted by faith, Rahab, the prostitute was not destroyed along with others because she received the spies in peace. Who is Rahab? Let's find out who this prostitute was. In Joshua 2:1-19, the bible revealed to us the wisdom of this woman in handling the spies. Rahab preached to them as if she was a preacher. Although a prostitute, she believed every word she declared to them.

"And she said unto the men, I know that the LORD hath given you the land, and that your terror is fallen upon us, and that all the inhabitants of the land faint because of you.

For we have heard how the LORD dried up the water of the Red sea for you, when ye came out of Egypt; and what ye did unto the two kings of the Amorites, that were on the other side Jordan, Sihon and Og, whom ye utterly destroyed.

And as soon as we had heard these things, our hearts did melt, neither did there remain any more courage in any man, because of you: for the LORD your God, he is God in heaven above, and in earth beneath.

Now therefore, I pray you, swear unto me by the LORD, since I have shewed you kindness, that ye will also shew kindness unto my father's house, and give me a true token." (**Joshua 2:9-12**)

In a nutshell, we have heard of what your God did, your God took you through Red sea, and helped you to conquer the kings of the Amorites. When we heard these, our hearts melted in us. *"for the LORD your God, he is God in heaven above, and in earth beneath."*

Why is it that we are not afraid of God, but unbelievers are afraid of God? God has become the one we treat casually, and He has become our mate. But here is a prostitute, who exercised her faith and pleased God.

"But without faith, it is impossible to please God, For he that cometh to God must believe, that God is, and that he is a rewarder of them that diligently seek him" (Hebrews 11:6)

Here was a woman, a prostitute, she had faith in God, and because of her faith, she was willing to defy her King. By that singular act, heaven marked Rahab, a gentile, and she was translated into the lineage of Jesus. This is very important, we need to understand the ways of God, and how God operates. There were two gentiles who should never have entered the lineage of Jesus. These were Rahab and Ruth. Incidentally they are in the same line, because Rahab was the mother of Boaz, and Boaz married Ruth who also was a gentile who entered the lineage of Jesus.

We need to understand the principles of God. So Rahab who was a harlot and a gentile, but because she had faith in God, hung the scarlet thread, as she was instructed, as a mark of her safety

"Behold, when we come into the land, thou shalt bind this line of scarlet thread in the window which thou didst let us down by: and thou shalt bring thy father, and thy mother, and thy brethren, and all thy father's household, home unto thee." (Joshua 2:18)

The scarlet thread represents the blood of Jesus. The scarlet is deep red, so scarlet red symbolically was speaking about the blood of Jesus, so what the spies were saying to the lady was, when we come back to destroy the city of Jericho, when we see the blood we will pass over you. Truly indeed when you go down to chapter six, you will see that when they did come, and the walls of Jericho sank the scarlet thread was already hung there. In fact, Joshua said, you two spies go quickly pick up Rahab and her family wherever that scarlet thread was and bring them to the camp of Israel.

That is what happened, when the walls of Jericho came down, the two spies went, picked up Rahab and her family, brought them into the camp of Israel, but God was not done yet. God said Rahab, because you believed me, I will not only save you, but I will move you into the lineage of the Lord Jesus Christ. And Rahab became the mother of Boaz, and Boaz married Ruth who also was a gentile.

Now let me show you a third gentile. Remember the woman that said, Jesus heal my child, and Jesus said healing is the children's bread and she said Lord when the children play with bread, some fall to the bottom of the table and the dogs under the table eat the crumbs. I pray you have faith in God, to be desperate to defy everybody and press in to obtain that which belongs to you. That woman was a gentile, legally she did not qualify, but because she believed in Jesus, she entered, and Jesus said, "**Woman, great is thy faith.**" (Matthew 15:28). Faith is the key, and that is why we are learning about the heroes of faith. In vs 32 to 40:

"And what shall I more say? for the time would fail me to tell of Gideon, and of Barak, and of Samson, and of Jephthae; of David also, and Samuel, and of the prophets:

Who through faith subdued kingdoms, wrought righteousness, obtained promises, stopped the mouths of lions,

Quenched the violence of fire, escaped the edge of the sword, out of weakness were made strong, waxed valiant in fight, turned to flight the armies of the aliens.

Women received their dead raised to life again: and others were tortured, not accepting deliverance; that they might obtain a better resurrection:

And others had trial of cruel mockings and scourgings, yea, moreover of bonds and imprisonment:

They were stoned, they were sawn asunder, were tempted, were slain with the sword: they wandered about in sheepskins and goatskins; being destitute, afflicted, tormented;

(Of whom the world was not worthy:) they wandered in deserts, and in mountains, and in dens and caves of the earth.

And these all, having obtained a good report through faith, received not the promise:

God having provided some better thing for us, that they without us should not be made perfect."

This chapter was not finished because you belong to this book, and until your part is written it can't be complete. This is the reason some of them, even though they believed, they did not receive it. What does that mean? It doesn't mean that just because you did not get what you were asking God for, you don't have faith. If you heard that, that is not always true. The fact that you believe for what you haven't seen, God is happy with you.

Before Isaac was born, God was already pleased with Abraham, because Abraham already believed. That is the reason Romans 4, tells us Abraham staggered not in faith, so at age 100 years old, Isaac came.

There's a man of God who prayed for years for a relative to be born again. I think for twenty-six years, the relative never got born again, and the person died, but at his funeral, that relative got born again, does it mean he didn't have faith? He had faith he didn't live to see it but that relative got born again on the day of his funeral.

So just because, like some of these people they didn't get it as at when due, it does not mean they do not have faith. The bible says without us they will not be perfected; we belong to the company of these heroes of faith. You are a hero, because each of us faces the challenges of life. Is there anybody who has no battles to fight? I am yet to find anyone. We are all confronted by one battle of life or another but let me encourage you, there are battles to fight because you have faith. The proof that God has put something in you is revealed by the battles you fight.

It is all part of the design. The faith God has put in you must produce something, for instance Moses was destined to do something, so God had to put Pharaoh in his front. God had to put the Red Sea in the agenda for the children of Israel to cross. Joseph was destined for the throne; God had to put his brothers, the pit, Potiphar's wife, and the prison in his path to prepare him, before he got to the palace. David had to kill his lion, bear, and Goliath to get to the throne. Challenges come to promote us, and they come because of our promotion to the next level. So if you're facing a challenge don't be afraid. Follow the counsel of God in James 4:7 and you shall overcome:

*"**Submit yourselves therefore to God. Resist the devil, and he will flee from you** "*. It is well.

CHAPTER 7

Types and Levels of Faith

The Christian faith we observe is a glorious one. We are neither just one of many, nor are we an alternative, we are it. There is nothing in this world that you can compare to the God that made the heavens and earth. In John 17:3, the Lord Jesus said,

"This is eternal life that they may know thee, the only true God and Jesus Christ whom you have sent."

The only true God is the God that sent Jesus. Any God that has nothing to do with Jesus is a fake one.

So you must never be confused about who you are. You must be confident in your God, and let others know you are a Christian. I believe in Jesus, I know He's on my side, and therefore I do not hide the fact that He is my Lord and Savior. God does not and will never change. It does not matter the challenges you are going through, it is not bigger than God, neither would it faze Him out nor put Him under stress of not knowing what to do. I have crossed a lot of valleys, and climbed a lot of mountains too. In the midst of it all, I have seen God miraculously dissolve all of them in His time!

Even then I've been in challenges where I doubted my faith, even as a pastor. The fact that you have faith does not mean you won't be challenged. In fact, the authenticity of your faith is proven by the fact that your faith would be challenged. If you don't have the anointing, the devil will leave you alone. The fact that you are anointed is the reason you fight battles. Since becoming a pastor, I've believed God for more grace; I have fought more battles in sixteen to seventeen years than in the previous twenty-five years of being a Christian. The battles I have fought within this period are unbelievably true and very real.

My experience left me with two things. One, I grew from one level of faith to another. My faith and convictions were sharpened as I went through those debilitating times. It drew me closer to God in trust and obedience, and sharpened my faith and inspired the audacity to take a stand for God who upheld me through the fire and the waters. Two, it opened my heart and eyes to the fact that I must have something in me the devil was after; if I was not dangerous, the devil would have left me alone since.

May I let you know that if you have no trouble in your life, it means you are not dangerous to the devil. That is why your faith must not move, any sign of your faith shaking is a red flag for the devil that you're insignificant. Your faith must be solid like that of Abraham who the bible says; he did not stagger in faith. They probably mocked him, saying "Old man! You are believing God for a child? You left idolatry and you want to follow God? And what has that gotten you now? By the way which God are you following? The God you cannot see?"

It's important at this point to examine the various kinds of faith for the purpose of clarity. Let's begin for example with weak faith.

1. Weak Faith

In order to understand what weak faith is, you need to begin by imagining the experience of Abraham when he encountered God. He was an idol worshipper, who had to leave after meeting the true God. He was strong in his convictions and he was not weak in faith that was the reason he did not stagger in faith. It is important at this point to let you know there are two types of weak faith. Romans 14:1 reveal the first one to us:

*"**Him that is weak in faith, receive ye, not to doubtful disputations.**"*

This category is about a baby/young Christian. So when somebody is young in the faith, they are weak in faith and it doesn't mean they are weak people. It just means they are immature, they don't know too much about God. They have not fought some battles yet. As a baby Christian God will not give you bones to chew, because you are at the milk stage, but you will not remain a milk stage Christian in Jesus name. AMEN.

The second category is the type of Christian who refuses to grow in faith, by moving from the milk stage to meat stage. The obvious problem in the church today is that, as God tries to move the milk Christians from milk to meat stage they struggle with it and complain bitterly. They don't want to eat meat, rather, they are still crying for more milk. Yet because they have passed milk stage, it can no longer sustain them. Whether they like it or not they must grow up or else disaster is knocking at their doors!

You must brace up for the demands of faith; there are mountains to climb and valleys to cross! It does not matter the battles you are fighting; God can deliver you. That's why in the church we must be careful not to kill our wounded ones. If a brother or sister has a problem, don't mock him, and don't laugh at her. That is not your duty, that is not grace and that is not the love of Jesus either. If a sister is weak in the faith, don't deride her. Don't kill her. At least, she still goes to church, just pray for her. Don't also give up on others too! Do you know why? The bible says,

*"**A bruised reed he will not break, and a smoking flax he will not quench; he will bring forth justice for truth.**"* (Isaiah 42:3).

The weakest Christian is more important to God than the strongest unbeliever. Let me repeat, the weakest Christian is more dangerous to the devil than the unbeliever. At least, he or she is a Christian, and is in the faith, and believes in Jesus. If you believe in Jesus, I don't care about whatever challenges you may be facing now because you are destined to win in Jesus name, Amen! So, don't let the devil laugh at you, telling you, "I thought you call yourself a Christian," Tell the devil: "Shut up! Shut the devil up and kick him out of your spiritual space!"

But what are we supposed to do in church? We are to receive weak Christians; we are not to kill or destroy them. We are supposed to help them. We are to help one another that is why the bible says in James 5:16: *"Confess your faults one to another and pray one for another, that ye may be healed."*

It ought to be that if anyone of us is struggling in the church, those of us that are stronger, are the people to help them. So, that's what we are expected to do, for those who are weak, who are immature, and who might be struggling in their faith. So in a nutshell weak faith is defined in the life of:

i. An immature Christian,
ii. A Christian who doubts the word of God, and believes circumstances rather than the bible.
iii. A Christian who believes the words of men more than the word of God (Bible).

When you believe the words of man more than the bible, then you are weak in faith. Conversely, let us now examine strong faith

2. Strong Faith

In Romans 4:19, the bible uses this word again, that Abraham *"... being not weak in faith, he considered not his own body now dead, when he was about an hundred years old, neither yet the deadness of Sara's womb:"*

What does that mean? In this case, it means Abraham did not lose confidence in what God told him. He held unto the word of God. We are weak in faith anytime we doubt the bible. I can tell you this, the bible can never fail. These scriptures can't fail. I know you will say: "Pastor, that person had cancer, they prayed and the person died. Yes, it is true, they died but that does not diminish the potency of God's word. The scriptures cannot fail. This is where the devil messes up Christians. We use our experience to try to define or explain the bible. That is the wrong approach. Flip it. We must superimpose the truth, veracity and infallibility of the bible on our experiences. You must choose to believe the bible more than what you are experiencing. You must shake sickness off your body. Keep telling yourself, *"By His stripes, I am healed"*. You might be having pains, it does not matter, but keep repeating what the bible says. Very soon you will see the result of your confession!

Before you were born, the bible existed. People have believed it. For thousands of years, men and women have believed the Bible and God has answered their prayers. You are also qualified in Christ to obtain results in your situation. This bible cannot change. If it worked for Peter, it will work for John.

The John I am sharing with you wrote the gospel of John, he wrote the Epistles of John, he wrote the book of Revelation. Do you know who that John was? Do you know that that John was put in hot boiling oil, and he did not die? This is history; it is not in your bible. It is the historical account of John the divine, John the youngest of the disciples. John the disciple that Jesus loved, he was the last to die because it was not yet time for him to die. He had to write the book of Revelation, so they put him inside hot boiling oil and he did not die. They were so shocked; they had to say this man is dangerous, this is not an ordinary human being. So they banished him to the island of Patmos. It was at the island of Patmos, he said:

"I was in the spirit on the Lord's Day..." (Rev 1:10),

He saw the Lord and he received the book of Revelation on the island of Patmos. Brethren, we serve a living God. So don't be weak in faith, it doesn't matter what your experience is telling you. Believe the bible, and read it every day. It works, this scripture is true. Men will change, but the bible will not change. Virtually all the prophesies about the return of the Lord Jesus Christ have been fulfilled. The only prophecy that perhaps has not been fulfilled is that everyman on earth will hear the gospel.

How can your faith be strong?

a) **It must be based on what is written, or spoken by God**. So whenever you are in a situation, your finance, health, marriage, job, and school work are under significant threat, it is time you go back to the bible and find out what does the bible have to say about success, prosperity, health, marriage, and life in general? What does the bible say about my protection? That the eternal God is my refuge, and underneath me are his everlasting arms (Deuteronomy 33:27). So anytime you fly, be reminded that the bible says, the eternal God, that means the God who has been, who was, who is and who is to come, who has no beginning, the eternal God, He is my/your refuge, not the pilot, but, the eternal God. The bible says underneath me/you are His everlasting arms. So it has to be written for me to be strong in faith.

b) **You must believe it.** God is as good as His word. When you doubt the bible, you are doubting God. You are not different from what you say. You are your word; you are as good as your word. God is as good as the bible that is why the bible says *He has magnified his word above his name (Psalm 138:2).* That means the bible will have to fail before God can fail. God has respect to what He has said, and made a covenant with us saying:

"I will not alter the words that have come out of my mouth." (Psalm 89:34).

That is why I must believe what God said. For example, He said to Abraham, *"...I have made you a father of many nations."* (Genesis 17:5). So how can you be saying you have no child? He believed God who quickened the dead and calls those things that are not as though they were. Abraham:

"Who against hope believed in hope, that he might become the father of many nations, <u>according to that which was spoken</u>, so shall thy seed be."

For believing in God's word he staggered not in faith. I like this verse so much because it is a word picture, and I just picture it because many of us in the church stagger in faith too much. The day you are happy, you come to church. The day you are not happy you sit at home. The day God blesses you, you bless God, the day He doesn't, you don't bless Him. The day you get a promotion, you have a testimony to share. Why can't we be like Abraham who come rain, and come sunshine, he had decided to follow God? We must be resolutely decided too like Abraham to follow Jesus without wavering. Abraham staggered/ wavered not in faith. ***You are not dangerous to the kingdom of satan, until you are unmovable.*** You have to be unmovable in order to deal with the wiles of the devil. You are the best of you, no one before you, no one after you. Don't try to be like others, be proud to be a Christian. Don't stagger at the promise of God. Let them make noise, let them laugh, but don't move, he staggered not at the promise, the promise spoken, the promise written, the promise spoken by God, but he was strong in faith.

That should be the response, the proof that Abraham was strong in faith, is hidden in those few words. *He began to praise God; he began to give glory to God.* Any time you are asking God for something, for whatsoever you desire, when you pray, believe, that you receive, and you shall have it (Mark 11:24) On a certain Sunday, I wanted to dance to the song "Shackles" by Mary Mary, but my heart was saying God has not done the miracle for you yet. So I wanted to dance but my flesh said to me why are you dancing? But the Holy Ghost said: "Can you imagine when it is done, what would you do?" Ah, I said "When God does it; I will declare Sunday for praise, so God said "Praise me now."

Let me ask you a question. How will you praise God, if He does something spectacular in your life? That is how you should praise him now and always. That's what Abraham did. That was the key and proof that he believed God. He gave glory to God, and he did not stagger at the promise. He was not looking at his experience, he believed the spoken word, and he believed the written word. Neither the fact that he had no child, nor the fact that Sarah had not given him a baby bothered him - he was unmoved by these.

3. Little faith happens when you are anxious, timid, fearful or worrying – Matt 8:26. A Christian has to have the ability to trust in Jesus and Jesus alone. I have been abandoned, I have been left alone, and we have all faced it. There will be times in your life; you will have to stand alone. Don't worry about tomorrow, God will take care of you? The Scriptures exhorts us not to "*be anxious for anything, but in everything by prayer and supplication, with thanksgiving, our requests should be made known unto God.*" – Philippians 4:6.

4. Great Faith

Do you know that before I proposed to Pastor Anne, she surprised me by acting in faith? She addressed one card to somebody, and put my name. So I said to her, "Sister, what of if I never proposed to you?" But you know in spite of that she believed that I was her husband. She had enough faith to see it through, and the rest is history. That she wrote my name on the card, still shocks me. That was part of the things I considered. This woman who could believe God and hold unto God, for two years, that this man is my husband, is authentic and real.

In Matthew 8:5-10, and 15:22-28 we see the Lord Jesus referring to two people, he said I have not found so great faith in Israel. He was talking respectively about the Centurion and the Canaanite woman. **Great faith** and yet they were gentiles, what was the key? They believed Jesus. One of the problems of Christians is that we become too religious. We think we know God, yet instead of looking unto Jesus, we look at our bank account, and conclude that God cannot do it! Who told you? God can bless you besides your bank account.

This is one reason when you go to crusades, some unbelievers get healed, yet born again Christians are there getting nothing out of it. Unbelievers get healed, do you know why? No religion, they just believe when the preacher says Jesus can heal you. They believe and they receive their healing. That was the secret of the Canaanite woman. She had heard about Jesus, her child was sick, and she came to Jesus desperate to get her daughter's healing. Are you desperate enough?

The bible tells us in spite of her desperation, Jesus answered her not. The disciples said Master *"...send her away; for she crieth after us."* (Matthew 15:23) Don't worry about the haters who say don't come to Jesus. Leave them alone Jesus didn't answer the disciples, what is their business? But she was persistent and cried louder. Then she came and worshipped him saying *"Lord help me"* (v25). Then the Lord said this is not for dogs but for children and in response, she made a profound statement.

"And she said, Truth, Lord: yet the dogs eat of the crumbs which fall from their masters' table..." (Matthew 15:27)

Her word of desperation divinely crafted, and wrapped and delivered with wisdom was the proof that she believed God. I am not asking for the main loaf of bread; the crumbs are sufficient for the dogs. I am humble enough to make do with the crumbs, Lord. Just one word said in faith changed the story of her daughter, and hers for good. Jesus could not hide His surprise and said to her: *"... O woman, great is thy faith: be it unto thee even as thou wilt. And her daughter was made whole from that very hour."* (Matthew 15:28)

Do you believe that one word is enough to save you? You don't need several days or months of fasting and prayer. She believed in Jesus that is why He said to her, great is thy faith.

In the case of the Centurion, after he told Jesus his servant was sick, Jesus responded by promising to come and heal him. In Matthew 8:8 we read:

"The centurion answered and said, Lord, I am not worthy that thou shouldest come under my roof: but speak the word only, and my servant shall be healed."

I am not worthy of such treatment, that you should come to my house, just speak the word only (the word of faith) and my servant shall be healed because I am a man under authority. One important point to note about both of them was that they approached and received their miracles on the platform of humility. They humbled themselves and heaven moved on their behalf.

The word of God went forth in both instances and their sick loved ones got their healings. Jesus never physically touched either of them, the word of God went forth to perform it (Jeremiah 1:12). The word of God carries power to do whatever you desire for it to do, if you can believe (Mark 9:23).

For example, many years ago in my high school, the President of the Christian group, was at the same time the Social Prefect. The school at that time wanted to organize a disco, and as the Social Prefect his involvement was required. They told him we know you are a Christian, and that you are not going to support this, do you want us to have this party? He said no, you are not going to. They said no, we are going to have it.

So defying his authority, they invited all the female boarding and mixed boarding schools in the city, and planned a big party. I was there. Saturday evening, the music was booming, the students waited and waited and waited, none of those girls showed up. You know why? It was because a child of God who was in the position of authority, and who had the right to approve of it, refused on the ground of truth.

That nobody showed up was not normal because my school was a very prestigious school, and every student wanted to be part of what was happening there. Every other time we had invited ladies they came, and we had parties between the schools, but on that day, none of the schools showed up. That is why you must believe, because there is power in the word of God in your mouth.

5. Mustard Seed Faith

In Matthew 17:20 the Lord revealed the fact that even a mustard seed size faith would move the mountain, if we believe. Faith has to be something that is living and active, albeit invisible. Mustard seed faith is not just figuratively a small or little faith, but a LIVING one. Faith is confidence in God, even if it is just a little confidence you have, the Lord says *"even if you have faith like a mustard seed, you can say to the mountain move and it will move"* (Luke 17:6). So there is mustard seed faith.

6. Faith to Faith

Your faith doesn't have to be big, but you must exercise, and grow it, and that is why we read in Romans 1:17 that we grow from faith to faith.

There are levels of faith, and you must grow in faith, confidence, and in your assurance that God is able. As a Christian, the only way to live is to live by faith. We must live by faith continually and not just for a brief convenient time frame. For example, in 2001, when the World Trade Centre came down, many people went to church the following Sunday, and three weeks later, they returned to business as usual and stopped going to church. Fear drove them to church in the first place. They didn't go because they knew God; they just went to church out of fear of death that is all. But the bible is saying the just shall live by faith all the days of their lives not just for a few days or months.

You must live by faith for the rest of your life. The righteousness of God is revealed in the fact that we grow from faith to faith. Your faith this year must be more than what you had last year, next year, let your faith grow stronger, that is the will of God, and that is the righteousness of God.

CHAPTER 8

Hindrances to Faith

Furthermore, in this study I want us to examine hindrances to Faith. The bible speaks about weak faith, strong faith, and little faith (Matthew 6:30; 8:26). So what is little faith? It is when you allow anxiety and worry to control you. These in themselves are hindrances to faith. Others include, doubt, unbelief, discouragement, and trying to reason God out and so on. These shall all be examined in this chapter going forward.

As human beings, we all face challenges that would cause us to be anxious. The reason is, when you are confused by worry, you cannot exercise faith. Let me share with you a poem or song on Why Worry?

Why worry, when you can pray?
Tell it to Jesus
And He will lead the way
Don't be a doubting Thomas
Just lean upon His promise
Why worry?
When you can pray.

1. Fear and Worry

What are the hindrances to faith? What are the things we must fight? Faith does not exist in a vacuum, you either have faith or you have the opposite of faith, which is fear. Faith is hindered by fear. That is why you need to understand that fear is a spirit, so you don't entertain it. Don't give room to fear in your life. Don't give place to foolishness either by doing something as dangerous as entering a lion's cage and believing you are acting in faith. Doing that would be tempting God. So when fear comes, reach out to God's word within you, and proclaim it.

You know sometimes it happens to all of us, when you feel pain and the next thing the devil tells you, is that it is heart attack. But you have to resist him to maintain your victory (James 4:7). Tell him devil, no heart attack in my body, I am healed in Jesus name. Don't give room to the devil through fear; it will hinder your faith, if you allow it.

Don't worry also, because eighty-five percent of what we worry about or fear never come to pass according to human statistics. That is why the bible calls the devil a roaring lion. The devil is not a lion, but he is like a roaring lion (1 Peter 5:8). He roars you are going to lose your job, and house. The devil is a liar. Your Savior is the true lion. So don't let anxiety ruin your life. Little faith means anxiety and worry. It also means you're timid or fearful; a Christian should never be timid. In 2 Timothy 1:7 we read that:

"For God hath not given us the spirit of fear; but of power, and of love, and of a sound mind."

2. Doubt

Doubt also is a subtle weapon the devil uses. He tried it on Eve in Genesis 3:1: *"...And he said unto the woman, Yea, hath God said, Ye shall not eat of every tree of the garden?"*

Did God really say you should not eat of every tree in the garden? You know that question was a very dangerous one. Did God really say it? The question was to sow or create doubt in Eve, and she fell headlong for it. If you are not confident about what you know, the devil will create doubt in you, and doubt is the result of little faith.

For example, when they encountered a storm of wind, they were sore afraid and woke Jesus up from sleep. He arose and rebuked the wind and said to the sea *"Peace be still."* The wind ceased and there was a great calm (Mark 4:39). And in verse 40 *"...he said unto them, why are ye so fearful? how is it that ye have no faith?"* Why are you afraid, don't you know that I am here? You have seen other things that I have done, why are you of little faith? Why are you doubtful?

This is why you must believe the word of God, and stop listening to the unbiblical counsel of your unbelieving friends. If you have a friend who does not honor God's word, please don't discuss your personal problems with him or her. If you do, they will dampen your faith, create doubt in your heart, and make you lose your standing in Christ. Believe God's word.

3. Unbelief and Discouragement are among the biggest hindrances we all face, but the difference is in the knowledge of the word we possess.

Don't be discouraged; keep trusting and following and you will overcome. The man who discovered electricity/light bulb failed 999 times, the man Edison, tested it the 1000th time and he got electric current. Don't be discouraged, no matter what, because you need courage to possess your possession. Every believer needs courage, if you don't have courage, you can't stand your ground, and if you don't have courage, you can't take what belongs to you. That is why in Joshua 1:9 God told Joshua:

"Have not I commanded thee? Be strong and of a good courage; be not afraid, neither be thou dismayed: for the LORD thy God is with thee whithersoever thou goest."

You need courage in order to resist the devil because he will oppose your promotion, and your attempt to enter your promised land.

Beloved, to leave Egypt is easier, than to possess the Promised Land. Therefore, you need courage to fight till you possess. Like Daniel, you need courage to continue to pray in the face of satanically orchestrated opposition. Also when he knew the time for the emancipation of Israel had come, he began to pray and fast and continued for twenty-one days. Even when the Prince of Persia withstood the angel bringing the answer, Daniel waited courageously in prayer. In Dan 10:12-13, we see the fruit or benefit of his courage reported to Daniel:

"Then said he unto me, Fear not, Daniel: for from the first day that thou didst set thine heart to understand, and to chasten thyself before thy God, thy words were heard, and I am come for thy words.

But the prince of the kingdom of Persia withstood me one and twenty days: but, lo, Michael, one of the chief princes, came to help me; and I remained there with the kings of Persia."

The answer was released the very first day, but the Prince of Persia hindered. Imagine if Daniel had called off the prayer session, a whole nation would have lost the benefit of his prayer! That is why we need courage because often times many of us have given up because of discouragement and we never possess what God wanted to give us.

You need courage, and what do you think David had? Courage. Why will Saul and David's brothers see a giant about ten feet tall, in Goliath and they ran away, because they had no courage! Everybody ran into the cave, but David said, what can be done for the person that can take this guy out? David had courage and that is why his faith was bold. If they say nobody has ever done it, there is a good chance that you can be the first person that can do it. You are told Christians can't make it here; you can be the first Christian that will make it. You have to understand that God with you is enough. He can open doors.

4. Cynicism

Don't be a cynical Christian. I feel so sad because I have seen so many in the church and they don't understand that there is no room for cynicism in the kingdom of God. Don't try to calculate God. I am a very intellectual person and very logical. I don't do things unless they make sense. When it comes to believing God, I suspend my intellectualism. I know what I am talking about because God taught me when I was a young man. I saw a lot of things in the natural, that didn't make sense. My only option was to trust him; I can neither analyze God, nor put Him in a test tube.

I love chemistry, but when I came out of the lab, I don't try to play God and say let me see. No, everything ends there in the lab, when it comes to God's word I know my boundaries and all I learn to do is to trust God's word. Don't be a cynic trying to reason out God. There are too many cynics in the church and we wonder why God does not do many miracles amongst us. Do you know why miracles happen in Asia and in Africa and not a lot happening here? The reason is because, we live in a cynical culture, into which some Christians have been unwittingly sucked into.

Christians in developing countries generally have no choice but to believe God. There are no state of the art medical services, so if you fall into serious illness, God has to come through for you to make it. This is the reason why there are more miracles in Africa. Don't be a cynic, and don't try to rationalize God. Doing this is the pathway to sin.

5. Sin

Sin creates a gap, because the moment you allow it into your life, it will dampen your faith. It is a strategy of the enemy; you think the devil just wants you to commit sin? No it is much more than that. The devil wants to dampen your faith; because it is not possible to live in sin and have faith. That is why living a holy life is important. Anytime you're living right, there is boldness, and confidence in God that you ordinarily do not have otherwise. The bible tells us in Proverbs 28:1 that:

"The wicked (i.e. the sinner) *flee when no man pursueth: but the righteous are bold as a lion."*

We have the accuser of the brethren, I mean, how can you live in sin and have faith? When you want to pray, the devil will come to remind you that you lied, and you know you lied. The presence of sin in anyone's life breeds doubt and fear negating faith in the heart.

6. Lack of Focus

A major hindrance to faith is distraction from and lack of focus on the Lord Jesus Christ. Hebrews 12:2 enjoins us to always look unto the Lord Jesus Christ, the author/initiator and finisher/perfecter of our faith.

Don't focus on the problem. Focus and act on the word. Anytime you act on the word, you activate your faith to produce a result. So the bible says Peter stepped out of the boat, on the word "**come**". As long as he looked at Jesus, he walked on the water. Peter physically walked on water. When he however removed his eyes from Jesus and focused on the waves and the storm, he began to sink. Anytime you remove your eyes from Jesus, you will see the storm, and when you see the storm, you will sink, and it will create fear, doubt and unbelief. So we see here that removing focus from Jesus to the storm and wind led to unbelief in Peter.

You must look to Jesus, no matter what. He initiated your faith and He alone can continue to sustain and eventually perfect your faith. Your focus MUST be on Jesus. He is the pattern SON and example to always follow. He is the word and the good shepherd.

CHAPTER 9

The Key Attributes
of Faith

This chapter discusses key attributes we can observe from the scriptures. Prior to discussing them in detail, I would like to lay a foundation on the idea of the necessity for living by Faith.

Now you hear a lot about faith. Faith is not just a specific area of the Christian life; it is the Christian Life. The Christian life is faith, and without faith there is no Christian life. The devil sometimes deceives many Christians because they don't understand the word of God. We brand some ministers of the gospel as Faith Preachers. There is no such thing as a faith Christian. Your either have faith or you are not a Christian pure and simple! So without faith, it is impossible to please God (Hebrews 11:6). So faith is a call to our relationship with God.

The Lord Jesus is the object of our faith. The object of my faith is a person. I am alive today because of Jesus. You have to know Jesus for yourself. Take the advice of Job in Job 5:27 and search out the truth for yourself and make good use of It.:

"Lo this, we have searched it, so it is; hear it, and know thou it for thy good..."

The question now is why are you a Christian? The Christian faith is based on a person, not a philosophy, it is based on Jesus, and your belief is not in man, but in the person of God. So everything I am sharing with you about faith relates to Jesus. The perception of many who have no more talking points to attack believers in Christ is that a Christian is just a person that is deceived or weak because he/she does not know what to do – and that Christianity is an escape route.

Today, an enviable list of professionals in medicine, law, engineering, banking, insurance, the military, the academics and building projects/construction and so on, profess the Christian faith. They are not Christians because they have nothing to do, but have put their faith in the risen Son of God, the risen Savior, and the one who was and is and is to come. He is alive for ever more, who from the beginning is God, before the beginning, He is. That is the object of my faith.

I don't have faith because I live in Texas, no or because it is a religious state. I have faith in God that made the heavens and the earth. Your faith as an anchor must be based on the Lord Jesus Christ who cannot fail.

KEY ATTRIBUTES OF FAITH

1) The first one which I believe is most important; is what I call the **hearing of faith**. The hearing of faith is in the present tense continuous. It is not just once or occasionally but a continuous hearing of faith. Many people go to church, but they either don't hear or choose not to imbibe what is said there. I'm not saying they are deaf but they don't hear in the spirit. The hearing of faith results in the acquisition of faith. That is how you can acquire faith, and grow your faith, and develop it.

"Faith comes by hearing and hearing by the word of God" (Romans 10:17).

For faith to come alive, you must hear with the hearing of the spirit and what does that mean? You don't just hear with your physical natural ear alone, but you must hear in the spirit, - the born again spirit must receive the word of God.

You must have an encounter when you are hearing the word; you must believe it because God said so, and not because the pastor said so. You must believe because of the God that can kill and make alive, that can destroy the body and destroy the soul. The God who said let there be light, so you believe there can be light. In effect, you must have a revelation/enlightenment of God, and of His will as revealed in the scriptures, you must have that revelation in your spirit. Having that revelation gives you an unquestionable assurance of His truth in your heart, which in turn inspires an inner strength that enables you to do exploits for God.

Daniel shows us the importance of the hearing of faith, when he still went ahead to pray as he always did knowing that he would be thrown to Lions. So what did Daniel know that you and I don't know? Why would a man know he's about to be thrown to lions, go home, open his window as he did before, kneel down and pray three times a day? Daniel was not moved. Where did that boldness or confidence come from? It came from his faith and the power of prayer. This is why what you are hearing as a Christian is important. So there is a hearing of faith that means you hear, with faith, and you believe in your heart. You hear because of the revelation God has given you. Indeed, your faith cannot grow beyond your revelation/enlightenment of God. We really need to know God for our own good. In line with this thinking Psalm 107:43 tells us: "***Whoso is wise, and will observe these things, even they shall understand the lovingkindness of the LORD.***"

The more you know Him the more your faith will grow. If you don't know who God is, you will not have faith. If we know the God whom we serve, we will not compare Him with man. God is not a human being. God is God all by Himself, and He is a spirit.

One of the reasons why many Christians don't have the hearing of faith is because when they hear, they try to rationalize God. You cannot rationalize God. God is not and cannot be reduced to matter, cannot be measured by time or limited/constrained by space; he can do anything, so when you hear His word just believe it. It may not make sense, believe it. The woman with the issue of the blood said:

"For she said within herself, if I may but touch his garment, I shall be whole." (Matthew 9:21).

Does that make sense? How can touching the helm heal you? But she had the revelation of who Jesus is. So she had the hearing of faith. She had heard about the miracles of Jesus and believed that the same will happen to her. She looked forward to the opportunity to connect her faith to receive healing by touching Jesus. In Galatians 3: 2 we read:

"This only will I learn of you, receive ye the spirit by the works of the law or by the hearing of faith?"

So Paul here was rebuking the Galatians who started in the spirit and began to walk in the flesh. He asked if their Christian walk, was based on works? Or is it based on faith in God? You were gentiles, you believed in Jesus and you got saved. Sometimes you may feel discouraged, that is understandable, but don't stay discouraged. Don't give up. But the devil may be telling you just take it easy, don't be a hardliner, and just follow God as much as you can. I don't care how long you've been Christian, don't give up.

You may look at your friends, your relatives and say everybody is doing well, God why am I having issues in my life? Know that the good works that God has started in your life, He will finish and perfect it. God does not start and not finish. God is the author, and the finisher; the beginning and the ending; the alpha, and the omega. The point is when you hear the word of God, hear it in faith.

2) **The obedience of faith**. Obedience to God and His word is the sure proof of my faith in Him. If I truly believe in Him to be who He is and what He does and what He says about Himself and His word, I would obey Him. The obedience of faith is inevitable. Obedience is imperative.

The reason many of us struggle in obedience is this, we don't believe in God. If you really believe God, obedience will follow. Faith produces a reverential fear of God in man. So here is obedience of faith, Rom 16:26

"But now is made manifest, and by the scriptures of the prophets, according to the commandment of the everlasting God, made known to all nations for the obedience of faith..."

This is the commandments of the everlasting God. This is made known to all nations for the obedience of faith. The reason people are going to go to hell, is not because they were the worst sinners on earth, but because they did not obey the faith, and refused to repent.

This command affects all men yellow, black or white, tall rich or poor, American, Asian or African, or European; it doesn't matter where you are. To all men, there is a command on every human being, everywhere, not only in Africa, not only in Texas, but everywhere to repent. The reason is mentioned in Acts 17:31, and it is because the everlasting God, the creator of heaven and earth. God: *"...hath appointed a day, in the which he will judge the world in righteousness by that man whom he hath ordained; whereof he hath given assurance unto all men, in that he hath raised him from the dead."*

This is the Obedience of faith. Every human being is commanded to repent. Repentance is a command that means you have to decide to change to follow Jesus. It is a decision you don't do for your father, your mother, or your children, you do it for yourself. It is a personal decision.

I decided to follow Jesus, it was my personal decision, when I became a believer and a disciple of the Lord Jesus Christ. Repentance is a decision. How did I repent? I thought I was a good guy, I didn't smoke, I don't do drugs, and morally well behaved, so I was a good guy in my own eyes. No, that's what many people think, but it's a lie and they are just religious. I was religious but I was not born again. As I looked at the mirror of the word of God, I was right in my own eyes, but in the eyes of God I was a sinner in need of repentance. The bible says:

"For all have sinned and come short of the glory of God."

The wages of sin is death, but the gift of God is eternal life through Jesus Christ our Lord. When I decided to give my life to Jesus; I did not know what was happening. Three months later I noticed a change in my life; this is what it means to be born again. That's what happened. So there must be obedience to the faith. Jesus is not optional. He says *"...I am the way, the truth, the life..."* (John 14:6). When I got home from school, I looked at my grandparents in the face and I told them, "From today. I will not join you to worship idols, I am born again, and I am a Christian." My grandparents said "But we all go to church", yes I said "We all go to church, but from today, I will not join you to worship Idols. I cannot be bending down and worshipping the god of Iron, and the god of the Sea. God forbid", I said "I am a child of God and from today, when you cook my food; cook it separately because I will not eat food sacrificed to Idols." If you are a Christian all things must become new.

As a Christian you should be a wonder to your generation, and your world. Don't accept defeat; don't accept the limitations of your life. When there is obedience to the faith, we can have assurance of faith. I call it the full conviction of faith. Hebrews 10:22 tells us:

"Let us draw near with a true heart in full assurance of faith, having our hearts sprinkled from an evil conscience, and our bodies washed with pure water."

Recall that at the beginning I declared that your faith is built on a person. The question is who is that person? He is God, who lives forever. Therefore, your faith can have assurance. In full conviction, let us draw near with a true heart, in total and complete faith. God existed before you, your parents, and great grandparents were born.

Do you know who how old God is? He is ageless. He is outside of time. God is unmovable, and you are supposed to be unmovable too. Be moved only by the word of God. A Christian that has to go far with God has to be dead to this world. He or She has to learn how not to be moved by what is seen, felt, or heard. There are a lot of voices out there, and that is a problem. We must key into the hearing of faith, but some people hear the devils. Let me give you a picture. Why do you think Jesus said to Peter? *"Get the thee behind me Satan"* (Matthew 16:23).

It was because even though it was Peter that we heard speaking yet it was the devil that was speaking through him. The Lord said I don't want to hear that voice because I have heard the voice of God. A body has been prepared for me. It is written in the volume of the books, for I come to do thy will oh God (Hebrews 10:5-7). He was destined to go to the cross and here was Peter trying to tell him, don't go to the cross. That was contrary to the mind of God.

The Lord Jesus rebuked that contrary voice although coming from Peter, because he was speaking a demonic word that was going to tamper with Jesus' faith. You must be able to do like Shadrach, Meshach and Abednego who stood their ground in the face of idolatry. They told King Nebuchadnezzar,

"...we are not careful to answer thee in this matter.

If it be so, our God whom we serve is able to deliver us from the burning fiery furnace, and he will deliver us out of thine hand, O king.

But if not, be it known unto thee, O king, that we will not serve thy gods, nor worship the golden image which thou hast set up." (Dan 3:16-18)

For many Christians, taking the kind of decision these men took would have been difficult. Their resistance revealed to me that they have a full assurance of faith, because they stood for God, and God stood up by them in the fire. They behaved like 'fully baked' Christians, who refused to break under tension unlike some of us whose Christianity is based on what we get from God. We know more about the hand of God, than we know about the face of God. When half-baked Christians do not see the hand of God, what do they do? They whine about imperfect situations in their lives.

Indeed, what if God does not give you what you want, will you still serve him? You must trust Him and be a fully persuaded believer at all times in full assurance of faith and not allow anything to separate you from the love of God (Romans 8:35 – 39).

3). **Word of faith**. The word of faith is the action of faith. It is the force of faith. It is the positive response to God's word. The word of faith is both the object of the faith and the basis of faith. Romans 10:8 tell us:

"But what saith it? The word is nigh thee, even in thy mouth, and in thy heart: that is, the word of faith, which we preach;"

It needs to and must be spoken and confessed/declared - Rom 10:8-10. Salvation and accompanying practical evidences, are usually the result of the spoken and declared word of Faith. We must learn to speak the word of faith like Joshua and Caleb.

What is the word faith? The word of faith is a person. The word of faith is Jesus himself.

"For in the beginning was the word, the word was with God, the word was God" (John 1:1).

Jesus is the object of your faith; He is also the basis of your faith. Because of Jesus, you believe in Jesus. He is the object of your faith, the one we are praying to, the one we believe in, and the one who also under-writes your faith. You have faith because of what He has done. You are what you are because of Jesus not because of the clothes you wear.

He is the object of my faith. Put your faith in God, for He is the object of your faith. When you are talking as a Christian, talk the word of Jesus. So if your child is sick, say "I command you - be healed in Jesus name, sickness go in Jesus name." It is done.

Don't say, "I hope this sickness will not come, or I hope this sickness will not kill somebody? I hope am not going to lose my job?" These are not the words of faith. You need money declare it and say "The Lord is Jehovah Jireh, He will provide." You have to see and believe the invisible to enjoy the impossible.

There was the story of a man of God. The wife said to him "Honey. No vegetable oil to cook at home." He said "Don't worry. God will provide." That is the Word of faith being expressed. In three days, someone from another city, representing a vegetable oil Company, sent a couple of gallons of oil to this man of God. The word of faith is true and real, you only need to speak it. Your tongue carries power, use it wisely.

What is the point about the word of faith? It is what we preach, you speak. You confess it because you believe in your heart. If you want to know the word of faith look at the Lord Jesus Christ. They told Him Lazarus is dead, what did Jesus say? "*He sleepeth.*" If Jesus says he's dead, he will remain dead. The Lord said he is asleep. So we are going to wake him up. The word of faith is going to wake him. In the case of the Shunammite woman, "How is your husband?" "It is well." "How is your son?" "It is well." Her son is dead, but she said what? "It is well." That is the word (confession) of faith.

Many times we use our mouth to destroy our miracles, because the bible says death and life are in the power of the tongue (Proverbs 18:21). Be careful what you say, like I always say to parents; never curse your children. Never speak negative words to your children. Let me tell you how powerful words are. Between the age of four and eight, I practically dismantled virtually all the toys bought for me. My grandmother and my aunty, who both were not Christians, would look at me, and say engineer.

At that age I don't even know who an engineer is. When I turned eight, I said to myself, I am going to be an engineer. I chose my career when I was eight years old. When I had this revelation one day it shocked me, I said what? So the words of my grandmother were that powerful to shape my career. Words are powerful. Let me tell you, every human being is a speaking spirit, and God breath into Adam and Adam became what? King James says "*a living soul*", but the original Hebrew text means "*and Adam became a speaking spirit*." It doesn't matter whether you are a Christian or not, because you are a human being, we have the nature of God in us. When we speak, they are creative. That is the word of faith.

4) **Quantification of faith?** The development of faith, faith grows, faith can be strengthened. The bible talks about the mustard seed faith, and in Romans 12:6 about the proportion of faith. So we know that faith can grow. There are levels of faith, so there is quantification there is a measure of faith. All of us don't have the same measure. The measure is how God has blessed us. We are all different; don't go about just imitating someone else. You see a guy buy a five-bedroom house and you say "I am going to buy a five-bedroom house too"; you see a guy buy a boat, you say "I am going to buy a boat too".

We don't all have the same measure of faith. It is very dangerous to do what other people do; you don't know where God has taken them through. Do you have any idea of the battles they have fought? Do you know how many devils, how many lions, how many bears they have killed? You want to be like David? Have you killed a bear, a lion, and Goliath? So everybody cannot kill Goliath, because there is a measure of faith.

So the bible says if you have prophecy, prophesy according to your faith. If God has blessed you with a gift, do it to your ability. Don't try to copy somebody else. Don't try to be like the Joneses. Why? There is such a thing as a measure of faith. Everybody is not at the same level; every person has a certain level, but your faith can grow, that is the point. But as at today, maintain your level. Aim to grow and develop in your faith.

Faith can be developed by continual use and exercise. By learning to exercise our faith at the level of the **Measure/Proportion** of our Faith and getting results, we are encouraged to trust God when faced with the next level of challenge. Faith anchored in God's word may albeit start as a mustard seed, but has the capability to produce results when exercised. Paul enjoins us to do that by exercising our God given gifts as part of our spiritual development - Rom 12:3, 6 and Rom 1:17.

5) **The spirit of faith** - 2 Corinthians 4:13. The spirit of faith is the force of faith. The spirit of faith is the power of faith. Faith is a spiritual force. It is not something you can see, but it is the substance of things we hope for, it is evidence of things not seen. But faith itself is not visible, just like God. God is invisible and your faith is invisible but you can exercise it because there is such a thing as the spirit of faith. The spirit of faith is like the spirit that operates in the church. It is the spirit that should operate in the church. In the church we operate by the spirit of faith. Not the spirit of unbelief. Not the spirit of doubt. We must have the spirit of faith.

6) In 1 Corinthians 12:9, the bible talks about **the gift of faith**, the gift of faith. That is the supernatural ability to believe God without doubting. The gift of faith is *"...sun stand still..."*, Joshua said, and the bible says, the sun stood still. That's the gift of faith. The gift of faith is exemplified in these words "Stand still ye children of Israel." The children of Israel left Egypt, they are heading to the promise land. The Egyptians pursued them behind, mountain on the left, mountain on the right, and the Red Sea was in their front. The first thing that

happened was that Moses said to the Israelites, "*...stand you still and you will see the salvation of God.*" (Exodus 14:13)

That statement was the gift of faith in operation. If you read the next verse, Moses began to cry. Moses came down to his human reality, but it's important to speak the word of faith to operate in that gift. When you say stand still you are exercising that faith required for a turnaround in your situation. Moses had earlier declared in part that: "*...the Egyptians whom ye have seen today, ye shall see them again no more forever.*" (Exodus 14:13)

This was a statement of faith in which he needed to have waited on the result, but Moses panicked and the human dimension of him took over. Please know that every Christian has two dimensions to them - there is the man of God dimension; and there is the human being, the natural person. That is why you pray, we are not God, but we have God in us, when we let God operate, we see the power of God.

So Moses says stand ye still, the gift of faith. But the next verse he is crying and God said Moses why are you crying? Stop crying, bring the rod, what do you have in your hand? Moses came back to himself; he had to operate in that gift of faith in which he already spoke. The gift of faith, allows you to believe God beyond what you normally believe. It is a gift, that every Christian can potentially exercise.

7) In Ephesians 6, the bible talks about **the shield of faith**, as a weapon. I call that the weapon of faith. So the devil throws words at you, throws ideas, throws advise and you rebuff it, you hit it back.

A Christian must know how to use that, because often times, the devil will barrage your mind. Why do people commit suicide? It is because of the barrage of the devil. Whenever you have negative thoughts, please do not create a room or house for the negative thoughts in your mind. You must rebuff it, we are not designed to be negative, and we are children of faith. So take up your shield of faith, you are not going to fail, you are going to succeed. Lift it up to bounce back all the doubt of the devil, so your faith is a weapon, it's a defensive weapon, often times, just because you believe, God will move.

Many people die not because of sickness; they die because of heart break, because they gave up. Many cancer patients survive because they had hope, they hold on. I am going to be alive and not die. The will to live and not die kept them alive even though they have stage 4 cancer. So faith is very important as a weapon, it's the shield of faith.

8) The bible talks about **the joy of faith**, Philippians 1:25 - the joy of faith. This is the joy that comes at the aftermath of answer to prayer or God's divine visitation. The joy that is inspired by His miracle. *A clear manifestation of our most Holy faith is the Joy of the Lord, that is part of our covenant right.* A life of faith is a life of Joy, as the Joy of the Lord produces strength in us – Nehemiah 8:10.

9) Galatians 6:10 talks about **the household of faith**. We are the family of faith, and Paul encourages us as a family of God to fight the good fight of faith. Every believer in the Lord Jesus Christ as Lord and Saviour are part of the Household of Faith, aka the Body of Christ, albeit particular members – 1 Corinthians 12:27.

Up to this point, we have reviewed the **hearing of faith**, the **assurance of faith**, the **word of faith**, and the **gift of faith**. We are to review shortly the **prayer of faith** and the **fight of faith**. We must learn the use of these faith weapons.

10) In James 5 the bible talks about **the prayer of faith**. Every prayer of the believer, must be the prayer of faith. A prayer anchored on the authoritative word of God, confessed and believed without wavering. This results in pleasing God when we come to Him based on the full assurance of the reality of His person and His subsequent action to reward those who diligently seek Him. The persistence in prayer activated from the heart is one that always produces a divine response,

as highlighted by the Lord Jesus Christ in the parable of the unrighteous judge – Luke 18:1-8. Often times we pray in unbelief.

If you don't really believe in your heart, don't pray. Build up your faith before you pray. For every prayer should be a prayer of faith. The prayer of faith, James says will heal the sick.

11) **Work of Faith**. Faith must drive your work for God. It must be the motivation of every work you do in the kingdom of God (1 Thess 1:3, 2 Thess 1:11). In living by faith, we must do all we do by faith. For whatever is done besides faith becomes sin – Romans 14:23. Our faith must always be accompanied by a corresponding action. One's confession, behavior and actions should seek to line up with the words of faith that we believe and speak.

12) Paul, in 1 Timothy 6:12 talks about **the good fight of faith**. The good fight of faith. The Christian life is a fight of faith. We are going to face challenges. The bible (Psalm 34:19) says many are the afflictions of the righteous: but the Lord delivers him out of them all. We need to understand the importance of this attribute of faith. The fight of faith involves both the defense of the Christian faith as well as standing your grounds in faith against all odds and adversities.

Too many Christians today can't fight. I don't mean put on your boxing gloves and box your neighbor. I mean fight the fight of faith. Why do we give up too quickly? Don't give up too quickly on your marriage, job, and academic studies. I know you failed the exams, repeat it and pass. Don't give up. There is a fight of faith. There is such thing called **the fight of faith**.

Do you know that Paul had a shipwreck? And more than once and do you know how many times Paul received thirty-nine stripes of beatings, thrice? He was stoned and left for dead, and God raised him up. He continued preaching. Some of us would have run away. He went to do the will of God; he was beaten and thrown into the dungeon. The bible says at midnight Paul and Silas prayed and sang praises. They did not whine or give up - they fought the devil to a standstill.

Why do we have to be the whimps in the church? Let me share a story with you. When I was in high school, and I became a Christian, we were severely persecuted by the school authorities. The Principal came one morning and said "Today the Christian group in this school is banned". That meant we could not even use our free time to meet and pray. We had a free time after dinner, dinner was 6pm the study time was 7:30pm, and so if you finished your food at 6:30, between 6:30 - 7.30pm we went to prayer meeting. Then the Principal said "Even during that free period, no more meeting".

The President of the Christian group who was a Prefect/Student leader came that afternoon to the dining hall before the entire student body and said "I know the Principal said this morning that the Christian group is banned"; he said "The Christian group is not banned." I am not telling you a fable, I lived through this. That evening we all went, and we had our meeting, and continued many weeks afterwards. One day the Principal and some teachers came, they saw us meeting. They looked at us and then they went away, and one time they called us into the Vice Principal's office, and we told him but sir, this is our free period, and that was the end of it.

Why should you say I shouldn't pray or meet? Let me tell you, a revival broke out after that. I learnt something as a young man - don't be afraid of people who can ONLY kill the body. Let me tell you, there is such a thing in the bible as an "*unrighteous decree*" (Isaiah 10:1). Too many Christians don't fight. This is one reason why prayer was taken out of our schools in this country. That's the truth, we gave up the fight. Tell me what should prevent you from praying during your free time? Tell me. It is an unrighteous decree. This is what the bible says,

"*Woe to those who decree unrighteous decree.*" (Isaiah 10:1)

That's why we pray for the government, because anytime they do something against the word of God, they put themselves under the judgment of God.

Fight for your marriage, and your job. How do you fight? Pray on your knees, there's power in prayers. The queen of Scotland some hundreds of years ago said this "I fear the prayers of John Knox more than all the armies of England." There is a historical documentation about John Knox! John Knox knelt down in the snow in Scotland, and said "God give me Scotland or I die" Instantaneously revival broke out in Scotland. I pray that the Lord would quicken us to fight the good fight of faith in our generation.

CHAPTER 10

Living By Faith

1. Living by Faith – The Manifestations of Faith

The injunction *"The Just Shall Live By Faith"*, discussed in Chapter 2, focused primarily on Foundational Principles about the necessity for every believer to live by faith. Living by faith goes beyond just the understanding of what it means. Living by faith must become a lifestyle and exhibit practically corresponding action, work and results. A life of faith produces results manifest for all to see. The Lord Jesus during his three and half years of ministry comprehensively demonstrated this especially to His disciples. It is incumbent on us all who believe to follow likewise and seek to live out our lives by faith in practice.

Firstly, living by faith begins with a personal decision to wholly and absolutely trust in the finished work of the Lord Jesus Christ. Accepting and receiving Him as our Lord and Savior (John 1:12) involves our hearing the preaching of the gospel (Romans 10:14), recognizing the grace that has appeared to all men (Titus 2:11), our obedience to the faith (Romans 1:5) and salvation by grace through faith in the Lord Jesus Christ (Ephesians 2:8-9).

Secondly, it is important to know who you have become in Christ. You are born again (John 3:6-8) and born of God (1 John 5:4) and of the will of God (John 1:13). You possess the divine DNA and are thus positioned to overcome the world despite all the tribulations that would come your way – Psalm 34:19. Paul further explains that you are now a new creation in Christ altogether (2 Corinthians 5:17). Your old self has been crucified with Christ and it is no longer you who lives, but Christ lives in you. The life you now live in the flesh, is lived out day by day by the faith of Christ and total reliance and trust on Him, who loved you and gave Himself for you (Galatians 2:20). Understanding this truth here, forms the foundation for living by faith as a disciple of the Lord Jesus Christ.

Thirdly, this new estate (new creation) and newly acquired faith represents a "spiritual baby" (immature) status, that needs to be nurtured and grown to maturity by the word of God (1 Peter 2:2). Your faith needs to be developed and strengthened continuously day by day by hearing the word of God (Romans 10:9-17). This will involve a process of acquiring, developing and growing in faith by delighting yourself in the Scriptures and meditating on them day and night (Joshua 1:8) and allowing it to renew and purge your mind of unbelief, doubt, fear and cynicism (Romans 12:2).

You must endeavor to live your life through the mirror of the word of God and allow it to be a lamp to your feet (day to day decisions) and a light to your path (strategic and futuristic decisions) – Psalm 119:105. As you learn and make every effort to do/obey and run your life based on the scriptures (Joshua 1:8), your born again spirit starts to get trained in faith and righteousness. In time and in whatever season and level you are in, living by faith starts becoming second nature as your life gets transformed (metamorphosed) more and more. Your life of faith leads you to maturity as you are able to prove what is good, acceptable and perfect will of God (Romans 12:2). Essentially, you learn to in practice start living by every word that proceeds from the mouth of God. In practice, living by faith is living by the word of God (Deuteronomy 8:3; Matthew 4:4; Luke 4:4).

Living by faith on a daily basis can be summarized based on the passage in Mark 11:22-24, where the Lord Jesus teaches us how to exercise our faith and continuously develop our faith 'muscle'.

2. Exercising our Faith   (Mark 11:22-24)

In order to exercise your faith you must adhere to the following expectations:

a) **Hear** - The expectation is that we are already hearing the word of God continuously. For faith comes by hearing the word of God. We must not be selective in our hearing, but learn to hear the whole scripture, whether it is convenient or makes us comfortable or not.

b) **Believe** – For anything we desire, when we pray, we must believe that we already have what we prayed for. We must learn to believe the whole scriptures as the inerrant word of God even when we do not fully understand or it does not make sense.

c) **Confess** – The evidence of our faith and belief that we have already received will be demonstrated by our confession. It is not enough to believe. We must confess what we believe. Our confession must be in agreement with both our prayer and our belief in receiving what we prayed about. With the heart we believe unto righteousness, but with our mouth confession is made unto salvation (Romans 10:10). We obtain what we have prayed and believed for, when we also confess.

d) **Act** (Works) – As we confess what we believe, in many instances, there must be a corresponding action to the prayer, belief and confession. If I prayed about healing, faith would require me to start behaving like I am already healed. Works/manifestation must accompany my faith. If I say I have the root of faith, the works (fruit) of faith must be manifested - James 2:17-18. Going through the foregoing practically will always produce the desired results of our prayers.

Storms of life will come. Things might happen to you that are unexplainable. All sorts of challenges might confront you. Through all of these, whilst living by faith, you would need to stand firm (2 Corinthians 1:24) and unmovable (Romans 4:17) by your faith in God and to stand firm in the faith you have believed in all these years (1 Corinthians 16:13) in spite of your circumstance.

Further injunctions to note as we live by faith in practice are as follows:

Don'ts of Faith

- Endeavour not to be weak in faith - Rom 14:1, 23
- Don't set aside or nullify or shipwreck your faith - 1 Tim 1:19
- Don't disown the faith - 1 Tim 5:8, 12
- Don't wander away or err from the faith - 1 Tim 6:10, 21
- Don't miss the mark and don 't overthrow/ undermine the faith of others - 2 Tim 2:18

CONCLUSION

This book in Chapter 1 begins with some apologetics of the Christian faith as "The Faith" and "Our Most Holy Faith". It continued in Chapter 2 with a comprehensive exposé of the phrase "The Just Shall Live by Faith" and using it as the basis for discussing foundational truths and principles of faith. The purpose and necessity for faith was the basis of the discussion in Chapter 3. Chapters 4 and 5 enunciated the concepts of the "Pronouns of Faith" and "Prepositions of Faith" respectively. The emphasis in Chapter 4 was that Faith is a personal thing that must be owned and lived out individually.

The idea of Chapter 5 was to demonstrate the tangibility and reality of Faith as a spiritual force to be employed in a believer's life daily. The discussion of the Heroes of Faith in Chapter 6 demonstrated Biblical examples of Men and Women who used their individual faith in a real and tangible manner to do exploits for God and in their lives. Through the Scriptures we do find evidence of the idea that there are types and levels/degrees/measure of faith exhibited by different people.

Understanding this principle and how it can be applied in our lives depending on the season we are, in our faith and walk with God, is the basis of the discussion in Chapter 7. Our individual and even collective faith can be affected by many factors that we need to be aware of, so we can develop mitigating strategies against them. Hence Chapter 8 focuses on the Hindrances to Faith. In maturing in our faith and exercise of it, certain key attributes from the Scriptures are noted and discussed extensively in Chapter 9. Faith, although an invisible force, always produces a visible effect. James argues that we cannot say we have faith, without the corresponding action of good works. Faith in practice therefore always produces a manifestation for all to see.

Chapter 10 hence focuses on the manifestation of faith in practice. It discusses how faith is acquired, developed, maintained and matured as the believer grows to become like the Lord Jesus Christ. The book concludes with the emphasis on the truth that biblical manifestation of Faith always works by God's love.

Final Word – Faith Works By Love – Galatians 5:6

In 1 Corinthians 13:13, the scriptures says *"And now abides Faith, hope and love, these three, but the greatest of these is LOVE"*. Furthermore, in Galatians 5:6, Paul firmly said that Faith works by love. God is love and everyone who loves is born of God and knows God – 1 John 4:7-8.

Clearly, LOVE, God's kind of love is the greatest and indeed greater than Faith and Hope. Love is the foundation upon which Our Most Holy Faith is built. Exercising, living and walking by Faith imperatively requires us to do so by Love.

Faith working by love consists of the intrinsic components below:

1. Faith is **Activated** by Love that is the love of God in our hearts. Perfect love casts out fear. The absence of fear helps to activate our faith in God.

2, Faith is **Energized** by Love – Once activated, our faith is further energized and powered by the love of God in our hearts. This love of God in our hearts continuously and consistently powers, strengthens and matures our faith.

3. Faith is **Expressed** by a revelation of the Love of God in us. Increasing revelation of God's love actively provides momentum to the expression of our faith in a significant manner.

4. Faith Works (produces results) by Love - For faith to produce results, it must be exercised in an atmosphere and soil of love. The Lord Jesus Christ in the Mark 11:25-26 passage concluded on the teaching of prayer and faith, by pivoting to the subject of forgiveness. He alludes here that praying in an atmosphere of unforgiveness will hinder prayers and desired results of what we are believing for. For faith to produce results, forgiveness and love must prevail.

FAITH WORKS BY LOVE.

Printed in the United States
By Bookmasters